THE BREAKER

THE BREAKER

HOW MEN CAN OVERCOME SHAME AND LIVE IN TRUE FREEDOM

MICAH LaCERTE
WITH DIANA CHALOUX-LaCERTE

The Breaker: How Men Can Overcome Shame and Live in True Freedom
Copyright © 2026 by Micah LaCerte

All rights reserved. No part of this publication may be reproduced, stored in a retrieval system, or transmitted in any form by any means, electronic, mechanical, photocopy, recording, or otherwise, without the prior permission of the publisher, except as provided by USA copyright law.

No patent liability is assumed with respect to the use of the information contained herein. Although every precaution has been taken in the preparation of this book, the publisher and author assume no responsibility for errors or omissions. Neither is any liability assumed for damages resulting from the use of the information contained herein.

Scripture quotations marked NLT are from the Holy Bible, New Living Translation, copyright ©1996, 2004, 2015 by Tyndale House Foundation. Used by permission of Tyndale House Publishers, a Division of Tyndale House Ministries, Carol Stream, Illinois 60188. All rights reserved.

Some names and identifying details have been changed to protect the privacy of individuals.

Published by Mission Driven Press, an imprint of Forefront Books, Nashville, Tennessee.
Distributed by Simon & Schuster.

Library of Congress Control Number: 2025927314

Print ISBN: 978-1-63763-488-2
E-book ISBN: 978-1-63763-489-9

Cover Design by Studio Gearbox
Interior Design by PerfecType, Nashville, TN

Printed in the United States of America
26 27 28 29 30 RR4 10 9 8 7 6 5 4 3 2 1

TRIGGER WARNING

This book contains detailed accounts of childhood sexual abuse, trauma, and the emotional aftermath, including descriptions of depression, anxiety, and suicidal thoughts. These pages are written with the intention of offering hope and healing, but the content may be distressing for some readers. If you're a survivor or sensitive to these topics, please proceed with care and consider having support nearby. Your well-being matters, and resources are provided at the end of this book to guide you toward help if needed.

"*The Breaker* is a courageous account of facing trauma, pursuing faith, and building a dream. Micah's willingness to speak openly about his journey offers encouragement to those who have lived with silence and shame. Above all, this book serves as a powerful reminder that healing is possible, freedom is real, and there is always hope."

Jeremy Vallerand, CEO and president of Atlas Free

CONTENTS

A LETTER TO THE BREAKERS – From Micah LaCerte   11
A WIFE'S PERSPECTIVE – by Diana Chaloux-LaCerte   15

PART I – MY STORY

1. Into the Nightmare   19
2. A Rocky Start   23
3. Easy Prey   27
4. Red Flags   33
5. Innocence Lost   35
6. Spiraling   41
7. The Breaking Point   47
8. Chaos   55
9. Chicken and Dumbbells   63
10. Public Service Announcement   67
11. Passion over Money   73
12. What's a Fitness Model?   77
13. The Crash   81
14. The Hitch of Myspace   87
15. Love in Las Vegas   91
16. Kansas City   99
17. The Fighting Cycle   105
18. World Champion   111
19. For Such a Time as This   113

20.	Transforming Lives	117
21.	The Vision	125
22.	The House	131
23.	COVID	135
24.	Pain to Purpose	139
25.	The "F" Word	145
26.	Lean In Level Up	149
27.	Finish What You Started	157
28.	The Call	161
29.	Hate or Healing	167
30.	Preparing for Battle	171
31.	Promotion Day	175
32.	Light on the Stand	179
33.	My Superpower	183
34.	The Breaker	185
35.	The Train	191

PART 2 – THE BREAKER'S WAY: MY STEPS TO HEALING

36.	The Healing Journey	197
37.	Step One: Say Something	203
38.	Step Two: Muscle Pharmacy	209
39.	Step Three: Securing Safety	217
40.	Step Four: Restoring Faith	225
41.	Step Five: Forgiveness	235
42.	Step Six: Mess to Mission	241

Epilogue: The One	247
Resources	251
Acknowledgments	253
Notes	257
About Micah LaCerte	265

The breaker [the Messiah, who opens the way] shall go up before them [liberating them]. They will break out, pass through the gate and go out; so their King goes on before them, the Lord at their head.[1]

Micah 2:13

A LETTER TO THE BREAKERS

To the men wrestling with shame: You are why I fought to heal. I know that weight. Shame eats you alive. It locks you in silence. It fuels anxiety and depression until you can't see a way out. I carried that load. It crushed me for decades.

Maybe you've known that darkness too, whether your shame came from a wound similar to mine—childhood sexual abuse that almost broke me—or from something else that burns just as deep.

A man I loved and trusted shattered me. He manipulated a boy, desperate for a father figure, and used a twisted version of faith to justify his sickness, leaving me with crippling shame, confusion, and anger at God for allowing this to happen to me. The mental, emotional, and spiritual impact of the abuse damaged every facet of my life.

I stayed silent for years. I buried my pain with work, pushed my body to the limits, and tried desperately to drown the guilt and worthlessness. Maybe you do the same? Maybe you numb your pain with alcohol, drugs, food, sex, or porn. Maybe, like me, you chased achievements or put on a mask that's so opaque no one sees through, not even those who are closest to you—the ones you love the most. Maybe your fix comes in the form of busyness. Stay moving and you can outrun the pain, you can drown the voices in your head, you can avoid the grief chasing you down.

But deep down, you know what I knew: Those fixes don't work. You can't outrun the pain. It will wait until you run out of breath and then it will pounce and sink its teeth into you like a ravenous lion. The bite marks look like addiction, depression, anxiety, broken relationships, job losses, anger, and emptiness.

I was stuck, drowning in shame, anxiety, and depression. Terrified that someone would find out what happened to me. Would they call me weak? Blame me? I thought sharing would strip away my masculinity.

I vowed that I would never tell. Most men keep that vow until the day they die and suffer their entire lives because of it. I thought silence made me tough. But I was wrong. Silence was destroying me, eating me alive one bite at a time. It robbed me of joy, stole my peace, and kept me shackled in chains of shame. It nearly killed me. I came close to ending my life to escape the pain that wouldn't relent.

It took massive strength, and tapping into the deepest levels of my God-given masculinity, to build the courage to speak up. When I did, the opposite of what I feared happened. I discovered I wasn't alone in this fight, and that millions of men and women have gone through some level of sexual abuse. Men often suffer in silence, which destroys them, and many end the pain by taking their lives. When I found my voice, I discovered that rather than making me less of a man, bringing the truth to light made me even stronger.

Vulnerability was my weapon. Speaking up meant facing the enemy army of my shame and charging onto that battlefield like a warrior akin to William Wallace in the movie *Braveheart*. I fought with all my heart and soul, and I not only built strength and resilience, but came out the other end a victor. When those chains of shame were shattered, I took back the joy, peace, and freedom that had been stolen from me.

This book is my story. I'll take you into the depths of my darkness, the most painful moments that I swore I would never reveal to anyone. It may be uncomfortable, and there may be times when you have to step away if something stirs up in you. Take the breaks when you need them, but come back. Because I'm not going to leave you stuck in that pain. What's more, I'm not just going to bring you to a place of pain tolerance or pain management and tell you that this is as good as it gets for you, the furthest you can go. I've got something more for you. This book will shift after I share my story. I'll take you through the steps of healing (with help from some of my expert friends) and the path of hope that God led me on to the life of freedom that I lead today.

Men, I'm speaking to you. I know that silence may feel like the only way. But I'm here to tell you that there is a different path. Vulnerability turns your pain into power. It takes tremendous strength to tackle your brokenness and wrestle it to the ground. It will fight back. It will growl, it will bare its teeth and try to frighten you away, it will lash out with claws that will likely land some blows and leave you with gashes and scars that will forever serve as reminders of the battle that you fought, and won. You are as strong as steel for stepping up and speaking up.

You are not a victim, and you're not just a survivor. You are a *Breaker*.

Trudge through the darkness with me, because in the end, we are breaking into the light together. I was an ordinary kid from Kansas. I went through something horrific that far too many kids have experienced. If I can break through, heal, and live a healthy, purposeful, and faith-filled life after the trauma of sexual abuse, I know that you can too.

Let's smash through the lies, demolish the chains of shame, heal together, and stand proud and victorious over the enemy we have mercilessly defeated. Join me. This is The Breaker Mission.

Micah LaCerte

A WIFE'S PERSPECTIVE
BY DIANA CHALOUX-LACERTE

When my husband, Micah, walks into a room, everyone turns to look. And yes, that is partly due to his physical appearance and big muscles. He is, after all, a world champion fitness athlete and multiple fitness magazine cover model. If I do say so myself, he's an eye-catching, good-looking guy!

But it's more than that. He exudes positivity and energy that draws you in. It's disarming. Any intimidation people may have is defused when his smile lights up the room.

When they look at Micah, they may see a highly fit, faith-filled, successful entrepreneur who adores his wife and is passionately dedicated to helping others.

What do they miss? Deep scars from ten years of childhood sexual abuse.

They don't see the hurt and pain he had to overcome to become the man he is today or the chains of shame, guilt, anger, fear, and anxiety that shackled him for years.

They don't see them because those chains have been broken.

I've had a front-row seat next to him as he's navigated this healing journey. We've climbed out of dark valleys to breathtaking peaks together to get here. It's been worth every step.

Micah is one of the strongest men you will ever meet, and I don't mean that because of how much weight he can lift in the gym. Building muscle takes time and doesn't happen overnight. You must lift heavy weights; when the weight is no longer challenging, you're ready to lift something heavier. This is what Micah has done in body, mind, and spirit.

To say I'm proud of my husband is an understatement. Words can't express how grateful, blessed, and honored I am to be his partner in this pursuit of positively impacting millions of lives.

Male survivors of sexual abuse often choke on silence their entire lives, fear and shame holding them back from shining a light on that darkness.

Micah's story is a loud and bright beacon of hope. His voice through *The Breaker* will help end this epidemic of silence; shatter the chains of bondage to shame, fear, and guilt; and set men and women *free* not only to survive but to overcome and thrive.

PART 1

MY STORY

1
INTO THE NIGHTMARE

I'm bigger now. I'm stronger now. Surely, it won't happen again.

I gritted my teeth and tried to shove the gruesome memories out of my consciousness as I sat gazing out the window of the train, speeding along from Kansas City to Washington state. I pressed my cheek against the large, cold window pane in the observation car and shifted my focus by straining to see if I could glimpse the front of the train.

The wheels let out a screech as we slowed and stopped somewhere in Colorado. New passengers boarded, including a group with kids about my age, in their early teens. A girl with sandy brown hair and a skinny, dark-haired boy came and sat at my table. I was grateful for the diversion from my thoughts. We struck up a conversation. They were on their way to camp and asked me where I was headed.

I lied, telling them I was going to stay with my uncle for the summer. It felt good to let them think that I was just a kid going to spend time with family. For a fleeting moment, I felt safe, unashamed . . . normal. There was comfort in knowing that they didn't know my story, what had been done to me, or the things I had been forced to do.

Their stop for camp came too quickly, and we said our goodbyes.

I leaned back on the seat of the train and stretched. The sun was starting to set, and I couldn't see much of the scenery flying by. I closed my eyes and tried to get some sleep . . . but my mind couldn't rest, drifting back to the last fight with my mother.

"I don't want to live here anymore!" I was livid. She was fresh off her second divorce, from a bully I despised, and the anger and disrespect I felt toward her were unbearable. Nearly every conversation flared into a relentless screaming match. I felt like she didn't care, she didn't listen, she didn't protect me. I felt like she only cared about herself, so I yelled and rebelled against any hint of authority she tried to assert over me. The fighting was nonstop.

"I don't want you living here either, you selfish, good-for-nothing brat," she had lashed back. She was at her wits' end. The frustration and inability to communicate with each other was exhausting for both of us.

I was a good kid for the most part. In any situation outside of home life I was obedient, respectful, and a non-troublemaker. But with my mother, I came unhinged. I couldn't stand it any longer. Or maybe she couldn't. Most likely, it was a little bit of both. I wanted out. She wanted me out.

That's how I found myself, at fifteen years old, alone on a train, heading to a home that would become the source of my darkest nightmares.

Kenny was waiting for me there.

Sleep evaded me as my mind roamed. Kenny had been in and out of my life as far back as I could remember. I recalled sitting with him on the swing set, playing ball, and the times that he made me feel special and loved, something I craved so desperately as a young boy with no father figure.

My body shuddered with disgust as a new wave of memories flooded over me.

"Come over here, son; I need you to do something for me."

I felt nauseous as I heard his voice in my mind, my eyes shot wide open, and I sat up straight in the seat, my heart beating fast at the memory of the last time I had seen Kenny, nearly four years ago now. A familiar panic mixed with shame and confusion shot through me like an electric shock as the train just kept rolling into the night, taking me closer and closer to him. My stomach churned, and I scanned the dim aisle for a bathroom sign, praying I wouldn't puke but wanting to know where to head if I needed to. It would be just a few more hours now.

As the night wore on, I found myself sitting in the dimly lit train car, anxiously chewing my fingernails as signs of sunrise started to streak across the sky.

Things would be different this time. They had to be. Right? This was the only way to get out of the living hell I was in with my mother. Wasn't it? It had to be.

I desperately tried to convince myself.

Don't let it in, Micah. Don't think about it.

I fought back the fear, desperately trying to shift focus to the excitement of meeting new people, being in a new environment, and, most importantly, the relief of getting away from my mother.

But the thoughts were flying faster and faster through my mind.

I was just a kid then. I'm much stronger than I was. He has four kids now, so I won't be alone. He's not going to mess with me. There's no way he would. His wife will be there, watching out for me. Mom wouldn't let me come if it wasn't safe.

As the train came to its final stop in Seattle, this is what I hoped. I was wrong.

2
A ROCKY START

Alice Cooper is my dad.

Okay, that's not the whole truth. But if you saw a picture of me and my father, when he is dressed for his role as "Alice" in his cover band, you would believe that he *is* Alice Cooper. The resemblance is remarkable. My dad is a real-life rock star with a true passion for music. He is a kindhearted and loving man.

My mother and father met in the 1970s through a mutual friend. My dad was fresh out of high school, and my mom was a few years older. She had been on her own since she was seventeen and worked for a housecleaning business.

There was an instant attraction. They started dating, fell in love, and tried to navigate life together as best they could.

After dating for over a year, my mom got pregnant. Whoops! It was an "accident," but my dad later told me with a little smile and a laugh, "Kids happen." Though I was loved, having me was a challenge in many ways. It brought massive strain to an already unstable relationship.

Saddled with immaturity on both of their parts, lack of trust, poor communication skills, unresolved trauma, and both of them doing things that hurt the other, their relationship was like mixing oil and water. It wasn't going to work.

After three or four years together, when I was just a couple of years old, things reached an unbearable point between them. They both gave up.

There's so much more to that piece of the puzzle, but, as it relates to sharing my story, this was the beginning of life without my father and the onset of a deep void that I desperately hoped to fill.

I was playing one-man baseball in my front yard one day when I was five years old. As an only child, I was always finding ways to entertain myself. With my T-shirt hiked up over my shoulders (I mean, I was showing off my abs even then!), I would throw the ball up as high as possible, keep my eye on that prize, and whack it with the bat as hard as I could across the lawn. I was focused.

I was *so* focused that a reporter from the local newspaper driving by saw me and pulled up. He asked my mom if he could take my picture. My mom complied, and I landed my very first cover photo, as they featured me on the front page of the next day's edition.

A happy kid, that's what they saw, and that's what I was for the most part. My mom and I had moved around a lot, finances weren't stable, and I was starting to question frequently, "Where is my dad?" But in general, I remember this as a happy time. That newspaper feature captured one of my last moments of pure innocence.

Seeing Kenny, you wouldn't have thought he was a pedophile.

He portrayed himself as a man of God. He was a leader in the church and had a loving wife. He was disciplined and kind and seemed to live a life of high morals and Christian values. Though he didn't have kids yet, he worked extensively with children at church and preschools.

My mom met Kenny and his wife through a mutual friend. In her mind, this was the perfect person to spend time with her young, fatherless boy and give him direction and guidance for life. Truly, this was an answer to prayer for a single mom and an only child.

Kenny seemed like a godsend. He took me fishing, we played in the park, we flew kites; all the things that an active, healthy little boy wanted to do with a dad, he did with me. He even taught me about Jesus, brought me to church, showed me how to pray, and taught me what was right and what was wrong.

I trusted this man. I loved him.

For the next three years, Kenny was a consistent part of my life, mentoring me, educating me . . . and grooming me.

3
EASY PREY

"We're dirty, Micah; we need to take a shower."

We were back at his house after a couple hours of playing ball at the park. I was exhausted and happy for the attention. I took my clothes off and got in the shower. He was naked and exposed in front of me. I felt strange, but I didn't know what was normal in a family. *This must be what dads and sons do*, I thought. The soap smelled manly, not like the flowery scented soap that my mom had. Kenny took the bar and a washcloth and vigorously spent time cleaning me, his hands groping all over my seven-year-old body.

For several years, sprinkled between taking me to church and playing ball, there were showers and times where Kenny would take me out in his old pickup truck. He always asked me if I wanted to drive as he placed me square on his lap. At the park, he insisted I sit on him rather than let me swing on my own. I was too young to understand what his physical arousal was. I didn't realize something terribly wrong was happening to me.

Kenny was looking for me. I checked every box that his predator instincts were searching for. He was on the prowl and I was easy prey. A young boy with a single mom, desperately looking for someone to come in and help make her life easier. I was a kid with no protector, vulnerable and naive from an unstable home with no father in the picture. I was perfect.

Things were changing in my mother's life. While Kenny worked his master-manipulation tactics on me, my mother was on the dating scene and had developed a serious relationship with a man named Robert.

After a year, they were ready to take the next step and get married. For the first time in her life, my mom would have a husband, and I was going to have a "dad" living in the house with me full-time.

Finally, my dream was coming true.

I remember seeing families with a mom, a dad, and a kid or more, all living in the same home, spending time together, doing life together, and I always wondered why I didn't have that. It was really all that I wanted: a dad, a mom, a family, a home.

I was happy to have Robert as a father. He would say yes when I asked him to play soccer or other sports with me. When I thanked him for playing with me, he would say, "Anytime, Micah." He was kind to me, and I felt like he loved me.

Along with this new relationship came a new home. In my mind, this was a dream home. It was a white house, the biggest one I had ever lived in because it had two stories! I had my very own bedroom, closet, and even a balcony just for me. My front yard faced the public park, with a merry-go-round, swing sets, and slides galore. Just beyond that was a creek, fully stocked with crawdads and frogs for catching and the perfect spot for wading, rock-throwing, and letting my imagination go wild, creating scenes straight out of a treasure-hunting movie.

Add to that the public pool diagonal to the park and the fact that I quickly made new friends in the neighborhood, and I was having the time of my life.

Having attended two prior elementary schools, one each for kindergarten and first grade, the thought of staying in *one* school for a few years and having the *same* friends for a year made me feel like the luckiest kid alive.

Kenny faded out of my life for the most part for a couple of years. He had moved to California, so he would make a random phone call checking up on me here and there, and that was about it. In hindsight, I believe this was his way of feeling out the situation and keeping a relationship intact in case more opportunities came for him in the future. I now understand that having stability, a family, a home, and a man who was looking out for me were all major deterrents for this type of sexual predator. With this newfound balance in my home life, I was a far less enticing target for him.

For some time, life felt normal. My biological father also came back into the picture, and though we weren't close, it was nice to spend time with him on occasion and know that he cared. I felt that my life was going great.

And then it wasn't.

I trembled with fear as I hid under the dining room table. I hugged my knees to my chest, covered my ears, and closed my eyes, trying to drown out my mother's screams. The tablecloth draped down just far enough to shield me from sight but not long enough to block the view of my mother being abused by Robert. The tears rolled down my face as I choked back cries of my own so I wouldn't be discovered. I felt helpless.

As a sober man, Robert was genuinely kind and loving, but it was like watching a transformation of Dr. Jekyll to Mr. Hyde on the nights when he couldn't elude the temptation of alcohol. His inner demons emerged, and he became a different person.

I didn't understand post-traumatic stress disorder (PTSD). All that Robert had seen and experienced as a Vietnam veteran plagued him on the inside, even when he tried to put on a happy front. When the painful memories and stress became too much, alcohol was his chosen medication, and his inner monster surfaced. I couldn't comprehend his pain, but what I could see was what happened when he drank.

The abuse grew consistently worse. I started to hate alcohol. In my mind, the negatives in my home were a result of that poison. It turned this man I loved into someone I didn't recognize. It destroyed my happy home, and it caused my mother heartbreak. I decided then and there that alcohol wasn't for me.

The divorce, though inevitable, devastated me. I lost a father figure whom I had grown to love. We lost our home and financial stability. My mother lost the love of her life. What hurt the most was losing the family structure that I had always dreamed of.

In the blink of an eye, I went from my private bedroom in the picture-perfect white house with the park in my front yard, to a small room in a battered women's shelter. I'm eternally grateful for these shelters. This space provided safety and comfort for my mother and me through this transitional time, but the feelings of sadness and loss were overwhelming during those first couple of weeks.

There was one silver lining for me at that first shelter. My eyes lit up when I walked into the playroom loaded with toys. There were trains, building blocks, action figures, Hot Wheels, and more. Aside from Toys-R-Us, I'd never seen so many toys in one place in my life. There was another young boy there; we became friends instantly. The play time with him was a welcome distraction, giving a sense of normalcy to a situation I knew wasn't normal.

We had to move on to a new shelter, and I was underwhelmed—not even a toy in sight. Thankfully, we didn't have to stay long, as one of my mother's friends offered us a temporary place to stay until my mom was able to get back on her feet and rent a small apartment.

The one thing that was consistent in my life was change: new homes, new schools, new friends. In my first eighteen years, I moved thirty times, went to three elementary schools, one junior high, two high schools, and lived in two states. It got to a point where I knew I wouldn't be in one place for very long, so I never got attached. I was excellent at making friends, but since I expected they wouldn't be in my life for long, it was easy for me to let them go. I didn't fear losing friends; I just knew it would happen, so I made the most of the time I had with them and replaced them with new friends as soon as we moved. Maybe it's not the healthiest way of viewing relationships, but it's how I coped.

I liked school because I always had a lot of friends, but academics were another matter. Reading comprehension was a struggle. Learning didn't come easily; I had to work at it, including taking special classes for extra help. Concentrating and paying attention for a long time was a challenge unless I was playing sports or working with math; numbers came more easily. I now know that my classroom challenges were linked to the trauma responses I was experiencing in my body, making focus and comprehension extremely difficult. I was a good student for the most part; I was trying to give it my best shot.

I wanted to do well; even at that young age, I wanted to be something more than what I had seen in my life. I thought trying my hardest at school would help me get to a better place someday.

Kenny magically reappeared after my mother and Robert divorced. I don't know if he contacted my mom or if she reached out to him. He still lived in California, but the phone calls started happening frequently again, as he was looking to fill that father's void in my life.

My mother invited the renewed contact, thinking that this positively influenced me. I was eight or nine years old and starting to act out at home, and the friction between us was growing. The fights were getting worse. Kenny started calling frequently to "be there" for me, to listen, to give me advice and guidance, and to let me know he was always available.

Looking back now, I know he had plans for me—sick plans. This opportunity to develop more trust and intimacy with me was exactly what he was hoping for. He just had to figure out how to spend time with me in person.

4
RED FLAGS

I gazed out in awe at the vast ocean before me. It was so big, so blue, it sprawled on as far as I could see. I curled my toes in the sand, sucked in a big breath of salty sea air, and gave a laugh as a cold wave crashed up and hit my feet and ankles.

Outside of a TV show or movie, I had never seen the ocean before. I always wanted to go there, especially after watching *The Karate Kid* and seeing Daniel LaRusso train on the beach to become the "All-Valley Karate Champion." And now I was here, standing on the edge of the Pacific, soaking it all in.

It was not only my first time to the ocean but was also my first time on an airplane and my first trip to California. It was December, just before Christmas. I was ten years old. I was so excited for the adventure that lay ahead on this trip.

Kenny had reached out to my mom with a generous invitation to have us fly out to California and stay with him, his wife, and their four children. I have no idea how this trip was paid for; all I know is that my mother said yes, and here we were in the land of sunshine and movie stars.

The trip started amazingly. I played with his kids, we made multiple trips to the beach, we went to their church, and I got to eat fresh oranges straight off the tree in their backyard. They were the most delicious oranges I had ever tasted.

I loved the church, mainly because they had a kids' choir, and the lead singer was the most beautiful little girl I'd ever seen. I had an instant crush. I just sat there and watched her. I thought she had the most amazing voice I had ever heard. She reminded me of the childlike princess from the movie *The NeverEnding Story*. The song she sang stuck in my head, and I would sing it repeatedly.

Things were going so well. I was having so much fun. I didn't want to go back home.

Our trip was coming to an end, and Kenny had called me into his room and told me to sit on the bed. As usual, I obeyed, but I immediately felt nervous as he closed the door behind him. A knot started to form in my stomach. I didn't understand what was going on. Had I done something wrong? Was I in trouble?

My mother burst through the door before Kenny could begin what he had planned. "Why did you bring *my* son in here and close the door?" Her voice demanded an answer.

I didn't know why, but a wave of relief rushed over me. Mom protected me, even though I didn't understand what she was protecting me from. It was a moment when I felt like my mother and I were on the same team.

I followed her out of the room, confused about what had just happened but relieved that whatever it was had been avoided.

5
INNOCENCE LOST

I hope she sits next to me.

Her dark hair and beautiful smile caught my eye when she stepped on the Greyhound bus.

At eleven years old, I noticed when a pretty girl was around, and although this one was at least twice my age, I hoped she would notice me too.

When she stopped at my row and asked if she could sit beside me, I said yes and gave myself a little celebratory fist pump on the inside. I motioned for her to have a seat.

"Where are you headed?" she asked.

"I'm going to see my uncle in California," I explained to her. Kenny wasn't my uncle, but it was how I referred to him, and it just made things easier.

I had been on this bus for over twenty-four hours, halfway through my cross-country journey. She was the first to sit next to me and the first to strike up a conversation. I was hoping she would think I was grown up, traveling by myself. That should impress her.

"Are you alone?"

I could tell she wasn't trying to pry but couldn't help her curiosity as to why a boy so young was on a bus all by himself.

"Yes," I replied.

We chatted a bit more, swapping names and making small talk about where we were headed and what we would be doing there. I was grateful she sat next to me, not only because I thought she was pretty but also because her presence gave me a sense of safety.

As grown-up as I was trying to be, there was a part of me that was scared. I was all by myself, hopping off the bus at various stops to grab some junk food from vending machines or the gas station whenever I got hungry and navigating the transfer from one bus to another. Yet there was another part of me that felt proud and brave. I was doing this alone; only grown-up boys could do that without a mom or dad.

Whatever suspicions my mother had about Kenny seemed to have diminished after that December break. Once we settled back into our routine, all concerns were forgotten.

Kenny reached out to see if I wanted to join his family as they moved from California to Washington state that summer, and I said yes. I was extremely excited about this adventure to see California, drive up the entire coastline, and stop at exciting places along the way.

That's why I found myself alone on a Greyhound bus for forty-eight hours, headed to Kenny, never expecting what he had in store for me.

This was already one of the best trips of my life. Before the trek to Washington, Kenny took his family and me to SeaWorld. I had never been to a major theme park before. I was captivated by the whales, dolphins, and games. I desperately wanted to win a two-foot Bart Simpson figurine, but after multiple attempts, it just wasn't my day.

With the boxes packed up, I piled into the van with Kenny's wife and their four kids, and we started the trip up the Pacific Coast Highway. Two days later, we arrived in Washington. The new home wasn't ready yet, so we stayed with some of Kenny's wife's family who lived nearby.

It was nearly sunset as Kenny and I drove to the new house. It had been a beautiful day, and he asked if I wanted to tour the home the family would be moving into. Of course, I wanted to check it out.

The house was dark. There were no lights, or Kenny just chose not to turn them on. He took me from room to room, explaining what each would be. There was no furniture, and I couldn't see much as the sun was setting and the home, filled with shadows, was getting darker by the minute.

The final room on the tour was a small bedroom. Kenny walked in and sat on the floor, inviting me to sit beside him. Something felt strange; a wave of anxiety passed over me. Thoughts of that moment last December in California popped into my mind. But this time, my mom wasn't here to protect me.

I had no reason to believe that Kenny would hurt me. I could trust him. This was no big deal; he just wanted to talk. My mind struggled to justify and rationalize what was happening.

I sat down next to Kenny, and he started talking. First, it was about the house and the plans for it. Then, the conversation took a hard pivot as he asked me about girls. Were there any that I liked? Was I starting to have feelings for girls? What did I think about when I thought of girls?

The happiness I'd had just a short time before dissipated quickly as I scrambled for answers. I felt awkward sharing with him, but I did because, after all, he was like a father to me.

I shared about a crush on a girl I'd met at the local skating rink. I had asked her to be my girlfriend, and I'd even given her a bottle of perfume.

Kenny listened and then shifted the conversation. He told me I would feel things that were much more than a crush very soon. My body was going to start changing. I was going to have sexual thoughts and urges. He also told me that God did not want me to have sex before marriage, so these feelings, these urges, were going to be a problem.

I listened, honestly not sure what to say. My discomfort was growing. These were things I didn't want to talk about. Why was he saying these things to me? Yes, I remembered hearing something about no sex before marriage at the church, but I didn't know why it was so important to have this conversation right now.

My heart started to beat faster. My stomach was turning in knots. I was confused. I wanted to jump up and run away, but I felt paralyzed, like I was in restraints, and he had complete control over me.

I tried to reassure myself that Kenny wouldn't hurt me.

I was wrong.

"God gave us a tool to battle those urges so that we don't sin and have sex before marriage," he said.

He leaned toward me and said, "Let me show you how it's done."

As the darkness consumed the room, this man whom I trusted and loved sexually molested me.

He violated me and defiled my innocence. His inclination for evil stole something precious and sacred from me. Something I could never get back. I walked into that house as one version of Micah; I walked out a completely different version.

My mind blocked out most of the details of that night; I don't recall the circumstances around leaving that room. I don't remember the conversations or what happened when we returned to the family. All I remember is the overwhelming feelings of disgust, shame, and guilt that engulfed me. I felt gross. If this was supposed to be a "gift from God," like Kenny said, why did it feel so utterly, horribly wrong?

Any reflection of what had happened brought on a wave of nausea and the urge to vomit. Sadness and confusion piled on. What would people think if they found out? What would happen to me? What would happen to Kenny? What would happen to his family? Maybe if I just pretended like it hadn't happened, I could forget about it, and it would all just go away.

I thought I would *never* tell anyone what happened. *Ever.*

6
SPIRALING

I kept my mouth shut.

The summer came to an end. We had fully moved into Kenny's new home, and every time I walked by "that room," I shuddered with disgust.

I flew back to Kansas City, still feeling confused and doubtful. I tried to rationalize his behavior. He was a godly man. All the people at church respected him. Maybe he knows more about these things than I do. Maybe every dad did this with their son. Even though I tried to rationalize, I still felt disgust and shame. I was relieved to get out of there.

On the outside, I looked the same. But on the inside, I felt like I was slowly dying.

I was back with my mom.

Did I tell her? Did I break that vow of silence and reveal the abuse to her? My trauma-clouded memories were distorted. Surely, I didn't, because something would have been done. The monster would have been stopped.

We were on the move yet again, from one apartment or home to the next, never staying for long. I was in middle school now, playing sports and making friends.

It was around this time that my mother found out about Big Brothers Big Sisters, an organization that connects kids like me with a "Big" who has volunteered to spend time and be a mentor. Thankfully, she signed me up for their program and I met my "Big Brother," a man named Bill. He was an entrepreneur with a nice car and a nice home.

This was the first time I had seen someone up close who was successful in business. I was inspired. For a year, I spent time weekly with Bill. I wanted to be like him. I wanted to run a business and have a nice car and house. Bill told me regularly that if I worked hard and worked smart, I could be and achieve anything in life. Hearing those words gave me hope. His life gave me a glimpse of a possible future of success. I didn't know how, but I was determined to be like Bill someday.

On the home front, my mother started dating a new man. As things became more serious between them, they started talking about marriage.

I protested. I could tell this was not a good man for her, and it wasn't a good man for me. But my mother ignored my pleas and, for the second time, married a broken man.

"Chicken Legs!"

Many times when I was within hearing range of my new stepfather, he started hurling insults. I was a skinny kid struggling with insecurity, and he knew it.

His digs were targeted at either my appearance or telling me how weak I was. I tried to shrug it off and act like I was ignoring him, that it didn't bother me, but it did. The words cut deep. I was already a wounded boy, now having to deal with verbal beatings every time I stepped foot in my home. I knew kids were bullies at school, but I didn't know adults could be bullies at home too.

I despised him.

In hindsight, I realize that he was a man who had gone through some trauma himself, never healed from it, and tried to hurt others to make up for what he was feeling inside. For years, I felt such anger and resentment for this man. But as an adult, I feel sadness for him.

Ironically, his favorite nickname for me "chicken legs" fueled my desire to start training calves at a young age. I didn't want skinny calves, and I wanted to be able to jump as high as my hero, Michael Jordan.

I would lock myself in my bedroom, stand on books, and do thousands of calf raises.

"Grandpa is dying."

My mom shared with me that her father, my grandfather, didn't have much time to live. Though she didn't have a close relationship with him or her family, she would go and care for him.

I couldn't understand. I was miserable in this home. Things were getting worse with my stepdad, and now my mom was going to be gone most of the time too.

I felt abandoned.

I barely knew this grandfather. I couldn't understand why she would leave me for a family she claimed had rejected her.

What was supposed to be just a few weeks ended up being several months of barely seeing my mother. I isolated myself. Dark feelings of depression moved in on me quickly. I would lock myself in my room, fighting the internal battle the only way I knew how and doing my best to evade the berating bully living in my home.

Kenny called frequently. He knew I was struggling, he knew I despised my stepdad, and he knew that I had no one to turn to and no one to step in and tell him to stop his grooming calls and put an end to these conversations. He would listen to me vent and then offer his support. Every time we spoke, he always managed to shift to sexual topics. He'd ask me private questions, insisting I answer him truthfully. I felt dirty, disgusted, and ashamed after every conversation with him. I would be mortified if anyone were to hear what we were talking about, but Kenny acted like it was normal and assured me frequently that God wanted us to discuss these things.

One night something happened that shook our already fragile household. My stepfather had a severe emotional breakdown. I was sound asleep when the sound of ambulance sirens and flashing lights woke me up. I wasn't sure what was happening, but it was chaotic and confusing, I was scared. The panic on my mother's face frightened me even more. I'm not sure exactly what transpired that evening, but that it ended up being the last straw in their severed relationship.

Another marriage ended. Another man was taken from my life. Even though it was one I didn't want there to begin with, it was still another family lost. My mom and I packed up to move once again.

The baggage from brokenness and trauma weighed heavier and heavier on me with each passing day. I didn't know how to carry it or how to process it. My relationship with my mother was rocky before, but the conflict between us escalated to new levels. I believe my mother had gone through trauma in her childhood and never dealt with it, resulting in an onslaught of mental health issues that impacted her life and my own.

We were both in pain; we were both struggling on the inside and didn't know what to do with our feelings.

I was angry. Every little thing was an argument. It was exhausting. We couldn't get on the same page, and it was to the point where we didn't even bother trying.

The brief reprieve I had from the fighting came during the time I spent with my other grandfather, my dad's dad. He acted as my chauffeur for baseball practices and games. He loved spending time with me and always expressed how proud of me he was. We had a warm and loving relationship that would grow and continue through my adult years. I was grateful for those moments with him that felt normal. I was just a kid, playing baseball, with his grandpa cheering him on. He didn't know all I was going through on the inside. He didn't know how his genuine love filled an empty void.

"I can't take this anymore! I'm going to kill myself!"

I raced up the stairs to my room and slammed the door shut before my mother could get another word in.

I flopped on my bed, buried my face in my pillow, and screamed as loud as I could.

I couldn't do this anymore. I hated her. I hated my life. I hated this home. The rage I felt on the inside consumed me. I couldn't hold the tears in. I started sobbing uncontrollably, my body shaking. I kept my face in the pillow so my mother wouldn't hear me and think she had won. I lay there for what seemed like hours and let the sadness and loneliness wash over me.

"God, please help me," I cried. I wasn't sure if He heard me or if He even cared.

When the tears finally stopped, I rolled onto my back and sighed. I looked at the Michael Jordan poster on my wall, my athletic idol staring back at me. I had to get out of here. I dragged myself off the bed and cautiously opened my bedroom door. The coast was clear, so I ran down the stairs, out the front door, grabbed my bike, and pedaled down the street as fast as I could.

I needed to think. I rode to the local basketball court, and thankfully, no one else was around. I picked the number one hundred in my head. I would stand under the basket, jump as high as I could, and try to touch the net a hundred times without stopping.

The physical exhaustion brought some relief. I sat under the hoop as I caught my breath.

My mind was racing. I didn't want to go home. I didn't want to spend another moment with her. She didn't care about how I felt. She didn't listen. She kept bringing these men in and out of my life; if I loved them, she ruined it. If they were mean to me, she didn't protect me. I was so sick and tired of my life. I felt like a caged animal. I wanted her to leave me alone, but I also desperately wanted someone to see me and love me. Maybe I would kill myself, I don't know how, but maybe I'd do it, and then she'd be sorry. Maybe then she'd regret treating me the way that she did.

I needed to get out. But where could I go? What could I do?

Anywhere would be better than here.

It had to be. I couldn't imagine a worse situation.

Little did I know that "anywhere" would not be better; it would be the worst hell on earth I could imagine.

7

THE BREAKING POINT

When my mother reached her breaking point, and I reached mine, she contacted Kenny to see if he would take me in. Kenny, of course, gladly obliged. He was eager to take on that father figure role in my life. Little did I know that being older, now fifteen, made no difference to him. He would have a prime target right in his home, with total control, and that was music to his ears.

I stared out the window as the Amtrak train pulled up to the final stop in Seattle. I took a deep breath, bracing myself for the impact of seeing him face-to-face once again while desperately trying to convince myself that things would be different.

I grabbed my bag and headed for the exit. *You'll be fine, it's a fresh start*, I reassured myself.

Kenny's family had moved into a different home; at least I wouldn't have to return to the house where he had molested me. My feeble attempts to calm my mind didn't work. The waves of fear, shame, and disgust washed over me as I stepped off the train and saw him standing there.

We drove up to the new home, and I breathed a sigh of relief. This was promising.

Kenny's family welcomed me back and made me feel right at home. I liked the room they had prepared for me, and there was a park just down the street with a basketball court. I knew I'd be spending a lot of time there.

I settled in, and everything seemed normal.

We attended church and weekly Bible study. They even signed me up for a teens' summer camp program. I connected with some local kids my age and made friends right away. I landed a part-time job at an auto-repair shop, so I was making my own money.

Things went well all summer. Kenny hadn't said or done anything to me, so I started to relax a bit. He wasn't going to mess with me now.

As fall and the start of school approached, I shuddered at the thought of returning home to be with my mother. What if I just stayed in Washington and went to tenth grade here? I had friends, Kenny's family seemed to like having me around, the baseball season was coming up, and I could try out for basketball in the winter. My mind raced with the possibilities of the year ahead.

I approached my mom with the idea, and she agreed without hesitation. I think this was a relief for her.

Next, I asked Kenny. His "yes" came with conditions. If I wanted to stay, I had to agree to step up and take responsibility within the family. I needed to help with the younger kids, do duties around the house, and do whatever he asked. If I agreed, I could stay, and he would even help me get in shape for basketball tryouts. It seemed like a great deal to me. I loved the kids; they were like siblings to me, and I felt like I was their big brother. I also didn't mind hard work. For me, it was an easy yes.

The alarm went off at 5:00 a.m.

I hopped out of bed, threw on shorts and a hoodie, and Kenny and I headed out for a morning run. When we were through, I showered, grabbed breakfast, and headed out to catch the bus to school.

Later in the afternoon, I headed to the park to work on my hoops skills. Kenny had created a series of shooting, dribbling, and passing drills for me to practice, and I went through them religiously every day. This became my daily routine. I enjoyed the disciplined schedule.

The big day for basketball tryouts finally arrived. Over one hundred kids were vying for one of about twelve spots on the team. I desperately wanted to make the cut. I gave it my all. I was one of the highest jumpers. I was a team player. I was coachable. I thought for sure I was going to make it.

On the final day of tryouts, there were twenty of us left. We went through drills, conditioning, and scrimmages. I laid it all out on the table, optimistic I would make it.

The following day, I eagerly approached the bulletin board at school with the list of names of all the guys who made the team. I scanned it. I didn't see my name. I must have missed it. I scanned it again. Nothing. It wasn't there. I hadn't made the team.

My heart sank. I choked back tears and held them in until I got home and could hide in my room and let them out. I was devastated. This had never happened to me. I had made every team I had ever tried out for. I was embarrassed. I felt like a failure. I had let myself down and feared Kenny would be disappointed. He had helped me so much, taken all that time to spend with me, and I failed.

I was crushed.

To my surprise and relief, Kenny wasn't disappointed in me. He consoled me and assured me that I had given it my all, and this would be fuel for me to work harder and get even better for next year. He would continue to help me. It was all going to be okay. For a little while, I believed him.

———

I heard a knock on my bedroom door.

It surprised me as I thought everyone had gone to bed. I was up finishing my homework and doing my calf raises, like I did every night.

I opened the door, and Kenny stood before me. He stepped inside and shut the door behind him.

My heart started racing. My body tensed as my mind flashed back to the last time he had me trapped alone in a bedroom.

"What are you doing in here?" he asked.

I was shirtless, wearing just my shorts, and I suddenly felt exposed.

"I'm working out," I replied. Thoughts were flying through my mind. What was he up to? What did he want from me? I was so sure that he was going to leave me alone. Maybe I was overreacting; perhaps he was checking in on me.

His eyes looked me up and down. A wave of nausea hit me; I felt dizzy as though I was going to faint. Fear gripped me, and I didn't know what to do.

"Good," he said. "You need to put some meat on those bones. You're so skinny."

I cringed at the word *skinny*; it brought up memories of the bullying I'd endured with my stepfather. But I kept my mouth shut. Maybe he would leave if I just kept quiet.

His gaze shifted, and he looked around my bedroom.

"Tell me more about this girl you like. Have you thought about having sex with her?"

Kenny had gradually been bringing sexual questions back into our conversations whenever we were alone. He had even gone as far as to share intimate and graphic details of his sex life with his wife. I didn't know what to say when he shared so explicitly. I was interested in sex and curious about what it would be like, but these conversations always felt gross and inappropriate to me.

I had cautiously shared about a girl I had a crush on at school, not wanting to go into detail with him. But here he was, standing in front of me, demanding that I spill every sexual thought I had.

I confessed my thoughts but insisted they were just thoughts; I wasn't planning to act on them.

"You need to pray about those thoughts; those will lead you to sin. God doesn't want that for you. But this is something you and I can do instead."

Kenny moved in closer, and that strange paralysis that I had felt all those years ago swept over me. I was terrified of saying no. I was afraid of fighting back. I fought back tears as he exposed himself, and the assault began.

I thought I was bigger now.

I thought I was stronger now.

Turns out, I was wrong.

My life shifted quickly from a dream to a nightmare.

The kind things Kenny had done for me that I thought were what a dad would do for a son now came with a price tag. The cost of a favor, like taking me to baseball practice or helping me buy a corsage for my date to the school dance, would be him fulfilling his twisted sexual fantasies on me. He made sure that no kind deed went unpaid.

As the weeks dragged on, I felt the darkness consuming me. I was in a state of constant panic. I felt like I was drowning. I didn't want to live. Depression and anxiety gripped me. Shame and grief, fear and confusion—there was so much happening within my mind, and I couldn't talk to anyone about it. I had to keep it all in. My life would be over if anyone found out what was going on.

I tried to pretend that everything was going great. I created an alternate world in my mind and tried to convince myself that it was my reality.

I had a girl crush. I was playing sports. I was working at my part-time job. I seemed like an ordinary fifteen-year-old boy. Yet on the inside, I was terrified every time I went home, every time I needed help, every time I went to my bedroom, knowing that dreadful knock on my door was coming.

Maybe I could kill him. If he were dead, it would stop.

One night, while he was driving, I thought about reaching over and grabbing the steering wheel. I could crash the vehicle into a tree or drive it off a bridge. Ending his life would mean ending mine, too, but at least the nightmare and the pain would be over.

He became bolder, more forceful, and more aggressive. Not only did he show up night after night in my room, but anytime we were alone together or driving somewhere, he would pull off the road into a dark corner or alley, assault me, and then act as though nothing had happened.

One night, he came to my room and did his worst to me. As he buckled up his pants and walked to the door, he turned and told me to memorize the first ten books of the Bible, and I would need to recite them to him the next day.

I nodded my head and agreed that I would. But inside, I was seething with hatred and anger—not just at Kenny but at God too. Why wasn't God protecting me? What had I done to deserve this? Kenny tried teaching me about God. All these other people in his life thought he was such a godly man, but was this what God was okay with?

Kenny's cleverness in controlling and manipulating the people in his life was masterful. He would give me just enough attention to make me feel he cared about me, perhaps even loved me. But then he yanked that love away, making me feel small and worthless. He convinced me that I was lucky to be learning all of this from him so that I wouldn't be a massive disappointment to God.

He manipulated his family too. Under the guise of "disciplined living," he kept all of them on a strict schedule, ensuring they recognized that God had made him the head of the home and that his authority was not to be questioned in the least. A regimented daily schedule for everyone ensured that bedtime curfews were enforced. He could then make it to my room undiscovered and unquestioned, night after night.

The double life I was leading was tearing me apart inside. I was reaching my breaking point. Something would have to give. I couldn't go on like this.

"Please, Mom, I have to come home now."

My voice trembled with desperation on that phone call. I was shaking, and I couldn't control the sobbing as I made my plea. I woke up that morning and knew I couldn't take another moment of this. I was shattered. All I wanted was to be away from here. To be rescued from this living hell.

My mother heard the pain in my voice and realized something was terribly wrong. She booked me a flight back to Kansas City as quickly as possible.

I sat staring out the window of the plane, a wave of relief flooding me. I was so grateful to be leaving. I wouldn't have to worry about Kenny coming into my room tonight. I had a pang of fear go through me too. I loved Kenny's kids like they were my siblings. I couldn't help but wonder if he would go to the boys' rooms instead. Would he start hurting them the way he had been hurting me? Did his wife know what was going on?

Guilt surged up in me. I was leaving them all. Who might be hurt next if I wasn't there? What if anyone in Kansas City found out what had happened to me? They would be disgusted. No girl would want to date me. No guy would want to be my friend. No sports team would pick me. If they knew . . . it would be the end for me.

I was in an emotional hurricane of shame, grief, depression, fear, guilt, and disgust. Six months after moving in with Kenny's family, I was returning to Kansas City, broken into a million pieces, feeling that this time the damage was beyond repair.

8
CHAOS

"What happened, Micah?"

When she picked me up from the airport, my mother frantically probed me with questions. As I sat next to her in the car, she could clearly see that her teenage son had changed, and not in a good way.

My spirit was gone, and the sadness was overwhelming. I was a shell of my former self. I could see the fear in her eyes and voice as she anxiously looked at me, searching for answers.

The thirty-minute drive home felt like an eternity. My emotions were high. I knew my mom needed answers, and I couldn't hold it in. I was sobbing, shaking, and choking on my words as I shared with her the horror of the past six months. Mixed with the emotion of sharing came a shudder of terror at anyone else finding out.

I can't tell you what went on in my mother's mind, except that she responded with rage, sadness, and tears. An appropriate response for the pain I had gone through.

She called to confront Kenny.

He didn't deny abusing me. But he convinced my mother that it was a mistake and that he would get counseling and, of course, never do it again.

So, rather than reach out to the police in Washington to file a report or even the church to let them know what had happened and that they had a predator in their midst, she left it at that and seemed satisfied that the situation had been resolved.

Maybe it just felt easier to let things go than to start the work of bringing charges against a child molester. Perhaps she truly believed that he was a man of God and would not do it again. Maybe she didn't realize the true extent of the damage done to her son. Perhaps she didn't recognize that, if he had done it to me, there were likely others. Maybe she was just scared. Whatever the reason, life just continued.

A part of me was relieved that nothing further had been done or reported. If my mother had told the police, people would have found out what had happened to me. I would be "that abused boy." Word would spread that I was damaged goods.

At that time, with my mind in a state of chaos, it hadn't occurred to me that this meant Kenny, a predator, was off the hook. He was free to continue hurting and abusing other vulnerable boys like me. Free to carry on his "godly man" facade at his church. Free to keep destroying the lives of others to satisfy his despicable cravings.

Had my mother turned him in, it may have protected other innocent lives from being shattered and broken. I didn't realize that our silence was a victory for him.

He won once again, choosing a victim—and in this case, a mother as well—who would remain silent.

Just breathe.

I desperately tried to calm myself as the panic attack began. My heart was pounding, it felt like someone was choking me, squeezing my throat so that oxygen couldn't get through. But there was no one there. My vision started to tunnel and blur. I needed air. An overwhelming sense of dread swept up and down my body, and waves of nausea sent me to the floor as I desperately tried to calm down.

The attacks were happening more and more frequently. They hit me anytime I was in a situation where I wasn't in control. I was triggered if I was a passenger in a car, or in a movie theater but not at the end of the row where I could escape easily. Elevators were a no-go; being confined in a small space with other people would set the alarms off in my ears. I quit playing competitive sports; the fear of being on a team bus without control was terrifying. Even if someone got too close to speak with me, invading my private space, it could send me spiraling into anxiety that I couldn't escape.

Soon after returning home from Kenny's, my mother set me up with a counselor. It was better than nothing, but I wasn't ready to reveal all I had gone through. Only bits and pieces. The rest I was desperately trying to repress and hide. I just wanted to be normal. To be like everyone else. The more I stuffed my feelings and repressed my emotions, the darker life became.

I didn't want to live. But the thought of following through and intentionally taking my own life didn't appeal to me either. I didn't want to do that to my mother, friends, or family. I couldn't kill myself. But if I were to get in a car accident or accidentally fall off a bridge and die, that would be fine with me.

I doubled over in agony as searing pain surged through my stomach. I bit my lip, trying to hold in a cry. The stabbing and cramping took my breath away. In these moments, I could only curl up in a ball and wait for the waves of torment to end.

The episodes of my stomach disturbances were happening more frequently and more intensely than ever. The doctors put me through a battery of tests, to no avail. They couldn't find anything physically wrong with me. But that didn't stop the onslaught of crippling pain.

Maybe the pain caused the anxiety. Maybe anxiety caused the pain. Perhaps it was both. My counselor suggested the stomach issues were a result of abuse-related trauma and that I could try breathing exercises and meditation. I didn't like the sound of either of those, so instead, I just did my best to avoid anything and anyone who would trigger a painful attack.

The anxiety consumed me to the point where I could no longer go to school. I became more reclusive and isolated. My solid 3.0–3.5 grade point average plummeted dramatically as missed classes led to missed exams, and days missed turned into weeks and months.

In my junior year, I wanted to graduate from high school, but after two months of missed classes, I was way behind. I knew I would need to raise my grades, but I couldn't sit through classes. The likelihood of having a panic attack was just too high. If this didn't resolve, there was no chance of me making it to graduation.

My mother found a program at the local hospital where I could complete my schoolwork in a private, controlled environment during the day. The day began with group counseling, followed by sitting in a private office where I could complete my homework. If I began to have an attack, there were professionals there to help me through it.

I kept to myself and didn't open up to any of the staff or other kids. I shared the symptoms of my abuse but nothing about the root of the issue. Some of the others questioned why I was even there.

During our group sessions, they shared about the things they were dealing with: alcohol, drug addiction, suicide attempts, depression, abuse, and more.

One morning, when it was my turn to contribute to the group, I just said, "My stomach hurts."

"Dude, just take some Pepto Bismol; there's nothing wrong with you," one of the kids jeered.

To them, it seemed pointless for a kid with stomachaches to be a part of this group of seriously troubled teens. The taunting didn't bother me. I preferred to take the jeering rather than let them know what I had been through. I enjoyed being a part of the group and them thinking I'd gone through less horrific circumstances. Even though that wasn't true, I wasn't there for healing. There was no way I could share with these kids what I had gone through. It was too shameful and humiliating. I would rather die than tell them. I just wanted to get my schoolwork done.

Between the hospital school and some night classes, I fulfilled all the requirements for eleventh grade and made it to my senior year.

Thankfully, the high school was willing to set up a system to help me resume attending classes. They knew I was a good kid and wanted to graduate and be successful in school, but I was struggling. The school gave me a card that allowed me to leave the school any time I needed to. If I felt a panic attack coming on, I just had to show my card to escape to a quiet private room at the school or go home. Ironically, I never used the card the entire school year. Just the thought of having that control and knowing I could leave if needed made me feel safe.

Take it one day at a time. That was my focus in my final year of high school. Thoughts of college and the future weren't pressing. I was trying to survive and get through one more day without the desperation and brokenness consuming me.

"Micah, I've got to go to the hospital."

I wasn't sure what was wrong with my mother. She was working on and off. Honestly, I was so wrapped up in surviving my own daily routine that I wasn't thinking about my mom's health or even noticing that something was off with her.

I spent a couple of nights with a friend so my mother could meet with her doctors, get a diagnosis, and then process what she was going through. She was having a lot of pain that the doctors attributed to fibromyalgia and chronic fatigue syndrome.

She stopped working when she said the pain was too excruciating. The fighting between us had once again escalated to the intolerable point. We were both struggling with so much trauma and pain, and neither of us knew how to process it in healthy ways. We took out our frustration on each other, compounding the stress each of us was going through.

She wasn't well. I wasn't well. I was grateful I was older now, and I avoided the house as much as I possibly could.

Bill was one of my best friends.

We met at school in the tenth grade and hit it off. His nickname was "Chill Bill" because of his laid-back attitude. He was, and still is, one of the best humans I've ever met. He got along with everyone. He was kind, fun, and easy to hang with. We both loved sports and stayed out of trouble. We played basketball and ping pong, we had jumping competitions (which I always won, lol), we went fishing and talked a lot about life. I felt safe with him. His presence gave me a sense of ease and normalcy that I didn't have at home.

I spent a lot of time at Bill's house and with his family. His mother, Patty; his dad, Tom; and his brothers and sisters were all loving and open-armed. When I was there, I didn't want to leave.

I don't know how she knew. But she knew.

"Micah, do you want to stay here for a while?" Patty asked me gently.

I don't remember telling her that I was struggling. I don't know if she could see it or sense a boy on the brink of disaster. But whether she knew it or not, she threw me a lifeline that day.

This family opened their home to me and treated me like I was a part of it. I finally had the chance to see how a healthy, loving family operated. I saw parents who communicated positively and lovingly with their children, even when they disagreed. I saw a family who had faith as a foundation of their home. At family dinners, we shared about our days and, better yet, listened when others told their stories. I did chores around the house, mowed the lawn, and contributed in every way possible. I felt safe and loved.

My panic attacks slowly subsided in this environment.

The structure I was able to build in their home provided a respite from the chaos of the prior years. I felt like I was in control in this setting. Amid my life's nonstop war zone, it felt like I had been airlifted out to a space where quiet and calm were possible, at least most of the time. The anxiety was still right there, under the surface. But I kept it at bay if I stayed in the ebb and flow of my established daily rhythm. The safety of Patty and Tom's home, with my best friend, Bill, always close by; the ability to drive my car; and the security of my "get out if needed" card from the school allowed my life to settle into a normalcy that had evaded me for years.

Though a lifetime of wounds wasn't healed, the consistency that living with Bill's family provided allowed me to get my act together enough to graduate from high school.

For the first time in a long time, I started thinking about my future, with hope.

I wanted to go to college. When I was playing sports, I dreamed I could get a scholarship for baseball or basketball. Those dreams were dashed when I quit playing due to anxiety and panic attacks. I didn't know where I wanted to go, what I wanted to major in, or what type of career I wanted to have; I just knew I wanted to go.

When Bill said he was going to Pittsburg State University in Kansas, I decided that's where I would go too. Thankfully, even with my spotty high school record, they accepted me. It was time for a fresh start. I was ready.

9
CHICKEN AND DUMBBELLS

Jean-Claude Van Damme was my idol.

The first time I saw the movie *Kickboxer*, I swore that I would look like him one day. I thought he had the ideal body for a guy. He was shredded, cool, always beat the bad guy, and always got the beautiful woman. I wanted to be like him—a super-fit superhero.

When I started at Pitt State, I decided to start working on my Van Damme mission. At six feet and 138 pounds, I wanted muscles, to be strong, and to find a girlfriend. It was time to take fitness seriously and figure out how I would build my body into something more.

I bought a membership at the YMCA and made new friends at the gym, which led to landing a job at the local supplement store.

The world of fitness ignited something in me. I remember seeing a copy of *Muscle & Fitness* magazine for the first time. I was hooked. I devoured every article and workout tip. I wanted to look like these guys. I wanted to *be* these guys. I finally had something worth working toward, worth living for.

I found a home in the fitness community, even in a small town. I went all in and engulfed myself in everything fitness. I learned how to eat to ensure that I was building muscle through my workouts. I needed a lot of protein, and I knew I needed to lift heavy weights, so chicken and dumbbells became the main staples in my daily life. Little did I know what a lifeline they would turn out to be!

I loved the gym and how I felt there, so I spent at least a couple of hours training daily. Something about the structure and discipline appealed to me. I not only saw progress in my body as I built muscle but also noticed that my mental state was improving. My mind felt balanced and less chaotic. I felt happy for the first time in a long time.

I spent far more time learning about bodybuilding and the world of fitness, nutrition, and supplementation than my college courses. I couldn't get enough. I'd bet that 75 percent of my time was spent on those topics rather than regular schoolwork. I poured countless hours into reading and learning as much as I could. I had found a pathway I was committed to following for the rest of my life. I dreamed that maybe someday I could own my own gym.

At the time, I had no idea the connection between mental health and exercise and how powerful strength training, in particular, is in combating anxiety and depression. Now, I know that God designed our bodies with an incredible capacity to heal, and we unlock that potential by training our muscles.

Muscle is the largest organ in the human body, and when called on to perform, it acts as a chemical factory for our body and brain. It's long been known that our brains produce chemicals such as dopamine, endorphins, oxytocin, and serotonin during exercise. These improve mood, give us a "happy" feeling, and combat depressive feelings. However, over the past several years, research has discovered there is far more to exercise and muscle contraction than we even realized.

For example, when skeletal muscle contracts, it produces hormones known as *myokines* that are released into the bloodstream.

Many types of myokines (also known as "hope molecules") impact different parts of our body. Studies show that some of them cross the barrier between our blood and our brains and act as antidepressants. Research today shows that exercise should be a mainstay in the treatment and control of depression and anxiety.[2]

Unknowingly, my dedication to strength training and this new lifestyle provided me with the most potent, all-natural, and effective medication possible. All I knew was that I felt better, and my confidence and belief in myself and my potential grew.

Within a year of starting this lifestyle, when I was a sophomore at Pitt State, the panic and anxiety attacks stopped. Without having to take a single medication for anxiety, and before really digging deeper into the healing I still needed, the episodes completely subsided from my life thanks to the fitness lifestyle I had stepped into. That, in and of itself, was a miracle. In my opinion, every doctor or therapist working with someone who has gone through trauma of any kind should be prescribing exercise as a significant part of their therapy. It is unbelievable what our bodies are capable of in terms of helping us heal from traumatic events.

The disciplined rhythm of my life brought mental, emotional, and physical freedom that I hadn't experienced before. I also learned that creating a rhythm in life, with order and predictability, is one of the best things for someone who has gone through trauma and abuse as a child. Dr. Bruce Perry, a brain scientist, conducted much research in these areas of "rhythm" and understood the power of structuring life so the former chaos felt controlled.[3] For me, that rhythm was waking up at 5:00 a.m. every day, heading to the gym, lifting heavy weights, fueling my body well, going to classes, showing up for my job at the supplement store, spending quality time with friends, and consistently learning more and more about health and fitness.

The impact that fitness had on my sleep was significant too. I'd suffered from nightmares for many years. It would feel as though

I were awake, even in deep sleep. Anxious feelings would take over me, and I would be in a state of paralysis. In every nightmare, I was trapped in one of the two rooms where much of my abuse happened. I tried to scream, but nothing came out. I tried to run, but my legs wouldn't move, and I felt like I was in a straitjacket. I would wake up drenched in sweat and terrified. I had gone to see a sleep doctor (who didn't know about my abuse) who advised sleeping in a room with complete silence and adhering religiously to a sleep schedule. That didn't help much, but when I began working out regularly, I was so exhausted that I started sleeping like a baby. Sleep is when our muscles repair, so deep sleep is essential to muscle growth. The impact the fitness lifestyle had on my brain eliminated the nightmares and allowed me to get the restful recovery sleep that I needed.

Fitness provided the means of relief for me, the "good feelings" that I know others have used drugs and alcohol to chase after. I had no interest in either of those. I had despised alcohol since the days of living with my alcoholic stepfather. I associated being drunk with being abusive and hurting people I loved. I saw that alcohol made people lose control, and the last thing I wanted to be was out of control. I had no problem avoiding alcohol, which was a blessing to my friends in college—I was always the designated driver whenever they wanted to go barhopping. With me, they never had to worry about staying out too late, because I needed to be home by midnight so I could stay on my schedule.

In the gym, I found solace. It was where I turned my life's negatives into positives. I crushed the dumbbells and, in turn, demolished massive amounts of stress. I had discovered a place where I served a purpose. And not just for myself. As both guys and girls started coming to me for fitness advice and tips, I realized I had a huge opportunity to help others make positive changes. And that felt good.

10
PUBLIC SERVICE ANNOUNCEMENT

"Micah, my name is Detective Brown. I need to meet you in person. We have some serious things to discuss."

A wave of adrenaline surged through my body; my heart started racing, and my cheeks and ears felt like they were on fire. A detective? What had I done wrong? Was I in some kind of trouble? My mind was racing, trying to make sense of what I was hearing.

"What is this about?" I asked him.

He answered me in an even tone. "I need to talk to you about Kenny."

Just hearing his name made me cringe. It had been four years since I had seen Kenny, and I thought I had done a great job shoving these memories far back in my mind. I believed I had locked them there and thrown away the key. But as those words came out of the detective's mouth, everything flooded back to me, all the shame and disgust. And worst of all, I realized that this detective was calling because he *knew* what had happened to me. This secret that I had guarded so tightly, which not even my closest friends knew, this guy knew.

As we scheduled an appointment and I hung up the phone, my mind spiraled. People were going to find out. What if I had to go to court? What if I had to be part of a trial and sit on a witness stand in front of people and admit what Kenny had done to me? What if it was in the newspapers? On television? Was I going to have to see Kenny again?

I felt a flood of relief on the flip side of those emotions. He had finally been caught. He wasn't going to be able to hurt other kids. At long last he would get what was coming to him.

Then, more fear and dread surged over me. The questions ran rampantly through my mind. As much as I had learned to control my emotions these last couple of years, in this moment, I felt like I was back at square one.

Who else had he done this to? Was it his boys? How many others? Was I going to meet them? Would Kenny go to jail? What if I told on him, and he didn't go to jail? Would he come and find me? Would he try to do something to me?

I thought I had escaped it all. I thought I was moving on. And now this.

As I drove the two-hour trek from Pitt State to Kansas City to meet with the detective, my mind wouldn't stop racing.

Detective Brown started questioning me, and as I answered, it felt like an out-of-body experience. I knew that it was me talking, but I felt disassociated sitting there, sharing the most horrific, gruesome details of what Kenny had done to me with this stranger.

"How did he get caught?" I asked.

A young boy in Washington, one of Kenny's victims, was watching TV when a public service announcement came on about sexual abuse. "You need to speak out to someone you trust if you've been abused," the message stated, while giving some examples of abuse. The boy turned to his mother and told her that Kenny, the man from their church, had done something like that to him. The brokenhearted, furious mother called the police and the church leadership, and, within no time, Kenny was taken into custody. I couldn't help but think this would have happened much sooner had my mother reported Kenny years ago. How many kids would have been saved?

Shortly after Kenny's arrest, both of his sons came forward, admitting that they had also been assaulted. Hearing this, my heart dropped. A wave of guilt engulfed me. What if I had just stayed? Maybe he wouldn't have hurt them. Perhaps I could have done something to protect them. This was all illogical thinking; this was guilt not meant for me to carry, but I couldn't help feeling the weight of it anyway.

Accusations against Kenny continued to pile up as three other children came forward. Kenny's wife was then asked to submit a list to the police of other potential victims. My name was on that list.

When the detective finished questioning me, he closed his notebook, looked at me sincerely, and said, "I'm sorry this happened to you." I fought back tears, but this time not because of the pain from the past but from the relief of someone hearing me, acknowledging me, and validating that what had been done to me was horribly wrong. He hadn't treated me differently because he knew my story either. He didn't mock me or think less of me. He never insinuated that if it had been done to me, I would do it to others. He didn't make me feel it was my fault or that I wanted it to happen. He made me realize that perhaps my fears of how others would respond were misconceived.

My fear of being a witness at a live trial lifted when the detective told me he had all he needed from me; the case was bulletproof between me and six other children who had come forward. Nothing was in the papers, nothing on television, nothing made public about the case. My secret remained safe. My story stayed in my hands to decide who I would or wouldn't share it with.

Kenny didn't fight the charges. He pled guilty to seven counts of child molestation and abuse. He was sentenced to fifteen years in prison. *Fifteen* years. If you divide that among the seven of us, he got a little over two years apiece. Two years in jail to cover the cost of destroying my childhood and almost destroying my life. *Two years.* That was the cost of someone stealing my innocence.

At the same time, as I ponder what seems like an insufficient penalty, I recognize that Kenny's case is rare. *My* abuser was caught. *My* abuser served jail time. Most predators are never reported. The majority get to live their entire lives with no consequence to the evil that they have inflicted. One reason is that most perpetrators are either a family member or someone close to the family.

According to RAINN (Rape, Abuse and Incest National Network), 93 percent of child sexual abuse victims know their abuser.[4] Only 7 percent of abuse cases are by a stranger. This has massive implications for people who don't share about their abuse. When it's someone you know, as in my case, you're less likely to tell. When it could disrupt your family life, or perhaps you're being threatened within your home, you're less likely to tell. There may be fear of not being believed, fear of shouldering the blame, fear of punishment, fear of repercussions. Fear is crippling in most abuse situations.

My emotions about Kenny's sentence were mixed. On one hand, I felt anger that the destruction of seven young boys' lives had such a small cost. On the other hand, I was grateful that he had been caught. I had a sense of relief knowing that he wasn't out there at night, in some little boy's bedroom, stealing his childhood and innocence as he had done to me.

With all the old wounds and hurts the detective had resurfaced, I was grateful for fitness. It was my outlet. When things got too heavy, I headed to the gym and lifted weights. I worked harder and poured more of myself into my passion for fitness. I did not know that soon, this thing that had been a lifeline to me would open new pathways and levels of success that I thought existed only in my dreams.

11
PASSION OVER MONEY

"Micah Shane LaCerte."

My heart swelled with pride as I walked across the stage to accept my college diploma.

As I heard the applause, I looked into the audience and smiled. I couldn't believe I had made it to this moment. It was one of those rare occasions when my mom, dad, and grandpa were all in the same place. The looks on their faces told me just how proud they were of me. I was the first person in my family to graduate college.

This felt like a massive achievement for me. Five years ago, I wanted to die, and now here I am, a college graduate with a new sense of hope and direction. I had earned a degree in business marketing, discovered my passion for health and fitness, and met one of the most important people in my life: my best friend, Nolan. He's been with me through thick and thin; he's like a brother to me, and to this day I consider him one of my greatest blessings.

I moved back to my hometown, and my dad and I thought it would be a great time to rebuild our relationship and get to know each other. He had a room available, so I moved in with him and my stepmother. I spent a year with them, and it was awesome. I discovered how much we had in common and what a gentle and hardworking man he was. I grew a lot of respect for my dad and started understanding why things had gone as they did when I was a kid.

I landed a job right out of college as an assistant manager at Sam's Club. It was the most money I had ever made, and the money was what drew me in initially. It was one of the busiest Sam's locations in the nation, so I gained experience doing many different tasks, from managing people to stocking shelves to handling customer service situations. I learned a lot but soon discovered that the salary didn't matter. I was programmed to follow my passion, regardless of the pay.

When people asked me what I wanted to do with my future, fitness was always the answer. It had saved my life. I wanted to help others transform in the ways that I had to.

I wasn't at Sam's Club for long; I knew I had to pursue the dream in my heart. I worked out at the local YMCA, so I approached them to see if they were hiring and if they needed personal trainers.

I sat in for an interview, and as the woman reviewed my work history, she said, "I see what kind of money you're making. We only offer ten to fifteen dollars an hour." She looked apologetic, but I didn't even hesitate. "No problem, I'm in!" I couldn't care less about the pay. I was going to work in the gym and start living my dream!

I started shadowing while gaining my personal training certification, and as soon as I was qualified to train, I started building a clientele. I had the chance to work with all types of people. My schedule got busy quickly. I wasn't making as much money as before, and I didn't care. I loved this.

After a while, I moved on from the YMCA and got a job at another corporate gym that paid a little more. I realized something about working as a trainer in a corporate setting: It was all about sales. It was all about client retention. It didn't matter how many personal training sessions you sold to a client; they wanted you to sell more. There was no discussion of client success, how much weight they had lost, or fitness milestones they had achieved. Those things were of no concern at all. Closing sales and retaining clients were the only things that mattered.

I wasn't wired that way. I wanted to help people transform. I wanted to teach them how to train and how to fuel their bodies so they could achieve the results they wanted. I remember thinking how crazy it was that people were coming to the gym and hiring a personal trainer because they wanted to lose weight or build muscle, but most trainers had no idea how to teach them to do this. They could take a client through a workout, but they couldn't teach them how to eat, think, and live so they could lead a long-term fit and healthy lifestyle.

Long story short, I wasn't a good employee. I was a rebel in that system because I was taking my clients through transformation. I was getting them to their goals and not trying to keep them as clients for life. Management didn't like this approach, so I didn't last in that setting.

It was clear that I would have to do my own thing to stay true to my passion. In the back of my mind, I remembered the words of my "Big Brother" Bill, who told me that if I worked hard and worked smart, I could do anything. His belief in me led me to believe in myself. It was time to start stepping into that dream of being my own boss and running my own business.

I got my first taste of entrepreneurship as I started marketing myself and building a roster of clients. I trained either in their homes, at their offices, or at a local track. Now, I could entirely focus on transformation. Granted, I didn't have a business plan. I didn't know exactly what route I was going to take just yet, but I had a solid foundation in marketing, so I was confident that I could create something of my own, put my degree to use, and make it grow.

12
WHAT'S A FITNESS MODEL?

Bro. I've been watching you for six months now. You are so disciplined in everything you do, and it shows! You should be a fitness model."

I had seen David Washington at the gym before, but we had never talked. That day, he approached me and gave me this compliment and advice, but my first thought was, *What is a fitness model?*

Dave and I ended up talking for over an hour, striking up a friendship that has stood the test of time; he is one of my closest inner circle friends to this day. He knew the modeling industry from his background as a dancer and entertainer, and he even had some connections that could help me, including a local modeling agency. He explained that fitness models weren't all bodybuilders or competitors; they were both men and women who were disciplined and in incredible shape, with great physiques as well as a marketable look. They could make money from magazine gigs, television commercials, supplement sponsorships, working at fitness expos, and more. They were paid to do what they loved to do anyway.

I was all in. This was it. I was going to be a fitness model. I hadn't thought they even existed in Kansas City. I'd never known one, but I didn't care. I was doing it. Dave's comment and our conversation stirred such excitement in me. I couldn't wait to figure out how I could be one of those guys in the magazines. This was the path to appearing in my favorite publications like *Muscle & Fitness* and *Ironman*. I called the modeling agency the very next day.

"Your pictures suck. You need new ones."

The agent barely said hello to me before those words came out of her mouth. I liked her immediately. This was the place for me. Brutal honesty and someone who would give me the advice I needed to make it in the industry. I signed with the agency that day.

The next step was finding a photographer who would shoot new pictures of me for free, so that I could start marketing myself. What I learned was that this was called doing a "trade." The photographer would do a photoshoot, you could use the pictures for yourself, and they could use your photos in their portfolio to show their work to others. I couldn't believe this was a thing!

My agent gave me a list of photographers to contact, and one of the names was a man named Will Patterson. We met and I shared my situation. We hit it off immediately. He had been shooting for years and was doing a ton of work with magazines. He saw something in me, he believed I had what it took to succeed, and so he agreed to do a shoot with me. But more than that, he submitted those pictures to some local magazines, and I landed my very first publications!

Will is another friend who is in my life to this day. We have done hundreds of shoots together. For years I even worked as his photography assistant, so I got to learn a ton about the modeling industry from the other side of the camera too. It was a priceless education that I am so grateful for.

My agency was very clear that there weren't fitness model gigs in Kansas City. That didn't dampen my spirits at all. I would be the first, I just knew it. In the meantime, I was going on tons of casting calls and booking many local commercials and print ads. At one of the casting calls, I met a producer who thought I would be a great fit for an upcoming reality television show. So before I knew it, I was off to LA to appear on one of the very first reality series, a show called *Manhunt* with Carmen Electra as the host.

My head was spinning with excitement from it all. I used this reality show to build even more relationships in LA, but I still wasn't making much money. Gigs would typically pay a few hundred dollars, and the income was inconsistent. I was struggling to make ends meet and pay my bills.

As a result of the reality show, I landed my first fitness magazine cover—the first one my agent in Kansas City had ever contracted. Later I landed a modeling gig for Hallmark and became one of the most popular Hallmark Hunk cards.

This was 2004, and social media was just starting to be a "thing." There were sites such as One Model Place, Model Mayhem, Bodyspace, and then the big one, Myspace. I had profiles on all of them and would share my successes. If you followed me there, you would think I was balling out and super successful financially. I was in a "fake it till you make it" zone. I knew this was going to lead to more. I knew I could use all of this to build something. I just didn't know what that something was. My mind was working on ways that I could use this momentum to build the business of my dreams and fulfill my passion.

The people I was impacting, and the people being brought into my life and impacting me, were healing me in ways that I didn't realize. My spirit, once broken by trauma and abuse, though not fully healed, felt alive with hope. I believed in a promising future.

I got a high from the accolades and success. I would compare it to the feelings you have right after completing a workout. Anytime I landed a new job or started with a new client, I had a surge of happiness and confidence. But what I started to notice was that it was short-lived.

As soon as the satisfaction of one success started to fade, I would sink back into familiar feelings of anxiety and depression. There was still healing that needed to happen, but I was avoiding it by chasing the thrill of achievement. The dopamine rush became a type of addiction. Since the high didn't last, just like any other drug, I constantly was searching for more success, more validation from others, more acknowledgment. Anything that would help me no longer feel small, weak, fragile, and shameful.

I worked incessantly. Working hard, whether it was in the gym or at my jobs or pursuing my fitness modeling career, kept me distracted from the pain I hadn't dealt with yet.

This system felt like it was working for quite some time. I thought that I had finally found a way to prove to others and myself that I was exceptional and worthy, and not in any way broken. I had hopes that these "upper" moments meant I was healed of trauma's impact.

But I soon recognized that any happiness I was achieving was based on the opinions of others. There's a saying, "If you live by their praise, you die by their criticism." I was building on a shaky foundation, one that could be knocked out from underneath me at any moment. And if that happened, what was really happening internally would be revealed.

I was surviving. But I wasn't thriving.

And then it happened.

It all came crashing down.

13
THE CRASH

The brakes screeched.

I caught a glimpse of the ladders falling from the truck in front of us onto the highway just before we hit them. In a split second, the car was tossed across the highway and slammed into another vehicle. The impact sent my body crashing into the door from my neck to my hip. I was in shock. I didn't feel the pain in that moment; the adrenaline was rushing.

As the car came to a stop, my heart raced. I did a quick mental check. I was alive.

My mother was in the back seat; her friend was driving the car.

"Mom are you alright?" I winced as I tried to turn my head to see if my mother was okay. Thankfully, she and her friend were shaken up, but no major injuries.

It was July 2005, and we were driving to the airport. I was supposed to be on a flight to Florida for some modeling opportunities. When those ladders flew off that truck, everything changed for me. Over the next couple of weeks, I realized that my injuries were more serious than I had thought. Pain radiated from my neck to my hip.

It wasn't getting better; in fact, it seemed to be getting worse. The positive trajectory I was on with my fitness and modeling career came to a screeching halt.

I had no health insurance, and I refused to take pain medications. Every morning, I woke up with debilitating pain. I was devastated.

I couldn't work out. The pain was too excruciating. My mental health medication, which came in the form of dumbbells and heavy training, wasn't an option. I lost my schedule and fitness opportunities, and I started losing the muscle I had been working so hard for.

Depression hit hard. The darkness I thought I had overcome started to consume me as I no longer had my coping mechanisms available. I lost heart, and mentally, I started to spiral.

"Micah, do you want a job?"

It was the owner of a local nightclub who was looking for a doorman.

I needed money and something to do since I couldn't train, so I said yes and was grateful for the cash flow.

Working in a bar brought back painful memories for me. When I would see people at the club who'd had too much to drink, it reminded me of my stepfather. I never wanted to be like him. I saw what alcohol did to him and what its effects did to my mother.

I was struggling with internal conflict, and even though I wasn't a fan of alcohol, I started having a drink here and there. A Red Bull and vodka to get me through the night and to feel like I was part of the scene. But this wasn't me. What was I doing? And more importantly, why was I doing it? Why did I feel like I had to fit in with the crowd?

I started struggling with depression and a sense of hopelessness. I felt like I was in a cycle that was getting me nowhere. My dreams had been crushed after the accident. I had lost a lot of weight; all the muscle I worked so hard for had atrophied since I couldn't train in the gym. I felt like that skinny kid again. I missed my fitness lifestyle; I missed the weights; I missed my early-to-rise, early-to-bed schedule. I knew I had to get back to it. But a part of me felt like it was all over too. Like my injuries had caused me to blow my chance of what could have been. Would I ever be a fitness model again?

One day I realized I needed a change. I quit the doorman position, completely cut alcohol out of my life (a commitment I stand by to this day) and started running the marketing and social media for a different club. It was a position better suited to me, and I was grateful, but I also wondered how long I could keep living a life that felt like it had no purpose.

"Congratulations, Micah!"

A friend from LA reached out on Myspace with this message. I was confused.

Congratulations? For what? What was she even talking about?

"I was at GNC and I just saw you on the cover of *Muscle & Body* magazine!"

Wait, what? I couldn't believe what I was reading. The cover? I hadn't done a photo shoot in over a year!

Two years prior I had done a shoot with a woman named Jennifer Nicole Lee. At the time, she had yet to establish a name for herself in the fitness industry. But since, she had become one of the most famous fitness celebrities on the scene. That photo we had done together was selected for the cover, and there I was, on the counter of every GNC supplement store in the country.

I raced to the store to see it for myself. It wasn't real until I had a copy of the magazine in my hand.

There it was! I bought as many copies as I could afford. The cashier looked at the magazine and then at me and asked, "Is that you?"

"Yes!" I beamed. I was elated.

As I stared at that cover, it reignited something in me. Even though my relationship with God was nothing to brag about at that time, I still prayed to Him here and there, and this felt like a message from Him telling me not to give up. Don't quit. Keep going.

It was time to get moving. It was time to push through the pain, both physically and mentally, and find my purpose.

I was focused. I still had pain from my prior injuries, but I discovered that one of the best things I could do was to get creative in the gym. I found ways to continue to get stronger while working around my injuries to reduce and prevent the pain. No matter my injuries, I refused to stop working. I was not going to be weak again. Weakness made things worse. I was not going to let life get me down again. I saw this as an amazing gift of a second chance. I wasn't going to waste it. I was going to come back stronger and better than ever.

I walked into Gold's Gym and signed up for a membership. Once I was checked in, I headed into the bustling evening scene on the weight floor. I soaked in the energy and looked around to get the lay of the land. I took a deep breath and smelled the iron from the weights; it was good to be in an environment that felt like home.

Even though I had lost twenty or thirty pounds since the last time I'd lifted a dumbbell and wasn't sure how much I could do, I felt energized. I had created a strength training plan to start gaining back what I had lost. Day one would be training my two favorite muscle groups, chest and calves. I headed to the Hammer Strength Chest Press and loaded it with my prior weight, but I could barely move it. I quickly realized this would be tough, but I wasn't deterred.

I lightened the load and pushed what I could, and then little by little, day by day, I started to rebuild my strength. I still had pain and issues from my neck and hip, but I managed my way through. I had some exercises and stretches I'd learned from a chiropractor right after my accident, so I incorporated those. I knew I wasn't likely to be pain-free, but it didn't stop me; I wasn't going to let the pain hold me back.

Something had shifted in me, and I had a motivation like never before. It was more than the feeling of motivation, which ebbs and flows depending on the day or mood. It was more profound than that. Motivation became a part of my identity, not just a fleeting feeling. Every day, no matter how I felt, no matter what was going on, I would show up, do the work, and get better. I was determined to become the strongest, fittest, healthiest version of myself.

With this newfound drive, I realized that this was going to be more than physical. Something inside told me it was time to start working on the deeper healing I had been running from. It was time to start doing the work on the inside. It was time to start facing those ugly wounds and deal with them rather than run away or stay so busy that I just didn't think of them. It was time to start lifting some of the heaviest "weight" I had ever lifted. And I'm not talking about dumbbells.

Looking back, I know that the "something" inside of me was a whisper from the Lord. He had a bigger plan, He had a bigger purpose, and all of the pain and trauma I had gone through would not be in vain.

I regained my physical strength, regained the traction in my fitness career, and took things to an even higher level. Opportunities started to pick up speed. Even one of my greatest dreams came to fruition when I had the opportunity to shoot for *Muscle & Fitness* magazine. I was finally one of "those" guys, the ones who had inspired me to begin my journey. Now, I was the one inspiring others.

I was feeling good, but this time around, I held on to the success more lightly, knowing that it might not last, and sensing that something deeper and more impactful lay ahead. I knew I wanted to help other people. I wanted them to understand how powerful going through transformation could be. I wanted them to see that it was about so much more than the changes on the outside. Yes, the body looks better, but more importantly, being healthy, fit, and strong positively impacts your mind, helps with mental health, and builds your confidence and ability to be better at everything else in life. *That* is what I wanted people to experience.

It was time to really dig in and figure out the blueprint for this concept. I finally knew what I wanted my business to look like.

Now I just had to build it.

14
THE HITCH OF MYSPACE

Myspace was *the* social media of the day back in the late 2000s.

It was awesome. There weren't limitations or algorithms like there are today on platforms like Instagram or Facebook. You could have as many friends as you wanted; you had a "Top 8 friends," which could cause a lot of controversy if you exchanged someone in or out. Your profile page could feature whatever photos you wanted, and you could even have your favorite song start playing anytime someone visited your page. You could build your friend list by sending out requests. I even hired a guy to send them out for me daily, so I easily built a following of over 150,000 people. But the *best* feature of Myspace was the ability to post inspirational or informative "bulletins." Basically, they were posts or blogs, but when you posted one, it went to *every* person on your friend list.

I was, and still am, a relentless marketer, so I was obsessed with this ability to market myself to land fitness gigs, showcase my success, and gain clients for my personal training services. I posted every single day, which meant over 150,000 people were seeing my content regularly, becoming more and more familiar with my name—or should I say, my nickname.

On Myspace, you didn't have to use your real name. Most people had some type of moniker instead. Mine was "Hitch." I had a reputation for being a bit of a matchmaker and had introduced some of my buddies to women who eventually became their wives. When the popular movie *Hitch* came out, starring Will Smith, my friends started calling me "Hitch" or "the Hitch of Fitness," and then the "Hitch of Myspace." I liked the nickname, so I started using it.

The branding worked. I would attend fitness expos, and people would start calling out "Hitch!" and want photos with me. Fewer people knew me as Micah everywhere I went and more people knew me as Hitch because they had seen my bulletins popping up nonstop on their Myspace newsfeed.

I had started sharing transformations of some of the clients I was working with in Kansas City. These posts included their before-and-after photos, the story of their time with me, the challenges they had overcome, the changes they had gone through, and what our journey together had been like. I quickly discovered that these stories and pictures were *powerful*. People just couldn't believe the changes my clients were achieving. I was inundated with people reaching out, hoping to work with me.

One morning, I woke up to a message from a woman in Canada.

"Hi Micah, wow, your clients are having such amazing success. I live in Canada, but I so badly wish I could work with you."

The light bulb went off in my head.

I told her, "What if I put together a plan for you, teach you how to eat and exercise, and you can check in with me weekly with your progress?"

She was ecstatic! "Yes! How much will I owe you?"

I charged her a minimal fee, and when the money came through my PayPal, I realized I may be on to something. If this worked, if she lost the weight even without training with me one-on-one, this could be the business concept that I had been searching for.

It did work. She ended up losing thirty pounds and then allowed me to share her transformation story.

This was amazing. My very first successful online personal training client.

Remember, these were still the early days of the internet and social media. People were blown away. What do you mean you worked with her online? What is online personal training? It's impossible to lose weight working with a trainer unless you're in the gym with them, right? That has to be fake!

But it wasn't. It was genius. And it worked. If someone followed the plan I put together for them, they could achieve great results, just as great as if they were working with me in person.

What would I call this?

Hitch Fitness? No, that was too long. Hitch Fit? Yes, that's it! The concept of Hitch Fit was born.

I wanted to teach people how to eat and exercise so that they could change their bodies by losing fat and building muscle, but more importantly, so they could change their mindsets and their lives. Now, I had a proven way to help people, even if they didn't live in Kansas City.

I shared the vision with one of my best friends, Adam Gross, who has been one of my greatest supporters for nearly two decades. He believed in me so much that he loaned me the money to get the concept of Hitch Fit started.

I had a new excitement and hope for life. I started to believe that the pain of my past wasn't going to keep me trapped forever. There was building to do, there was healing to do, but I was ready for it.

And then, just like that, when God knew I was finally ready to receive one of the biggest blessings of my life . . . along came Diana.

15
LOVE IN LAS VEGAS

"Wow, she's pretty."

That was my first thought when I saw Diana walking toward me at the Olympia Expo in Las Vegas with a beaming smile and ripped abs.

Her profile had popped up on my account several months earlier, and we'd messaged back and forth here and there, just friendly talk. We were both passionate about fitness; she was competing and shooting with various fitness magazines, and we had a lot of mutual friends in the industry. Our connection was instant and natural based on lifestyle similarities. We spoke on the phone once and had a great conversation. We were both on similar missions with a passion for helping others. She had gone through her own transformational weight loss journey and wanted to help others do the same, just like I did.

The Olympia in Las Vegas was the place to see and be seen. If you were in the fitness world trying to make a name for yourself, this is where you came to connect with photographers, magazines, supplement companies, old friends, and new ones. Walking around the expo was an event in itself—you never knew when you would meet someone who could be instrumental in your career or life.

Diana and I agreed that we would find each other at the expo to take a photo, and then I had plans to spend time with other friends from the industry whom I hadn't seen in a long time.

I was happily single. I wasn't looking for anything serious. I was focused on my career and developing the concept I had for Hitch Fit. I wasn't interested in a relationship, and I certainly didn't think that was the weekend I would meet my wife!

Diana and I posed for our first picture together, and something felt different with her. We had just met, but I felt like I had known this woman my entire life. I felt like we were best friends. It's hard to explain; it was just natural and easy. I know she felt it, too, because instead of the "nice to meet you and see you later" hug, we both hesitated.

"What's your plan for the day?" she asked.

"Hanging out with you," I responded.

She just smiled and said, "Okay, sounds good!"

We wandered the expo together for hours, getting to know each other.

At the end of the day, it felt weird to say goodbye. But I had committed to meeting up with some friends at a party, so we parted ways. That night, I couldn't stop thinking about her. I missed her. I couldn't wait to see her again.

The next morning, I messaged her to see if she wanted to go have breakfast. The answer was yes, and that started another full day together. I canceled all the plans I had with other people; I only wanted to spend time with her.

I had never felt this way before. Diana was different from any girls I had dated. First off, she was a two-time Fitness World Champion, so I knew our lifestyles were in alignment, and I discovered that she was extremely lucky, having won a car on *The Price Is Right*! She could get done up, but she didn't have to and didn't feel the need to most of the time. She was down-to-earth, strong and confident, independent, and a hard worker. When I spoke to her, I could tell that she was listening intently and seeing me for who I was.

We both realized this was more than hanging out for the weekend. Rather than going to the Olympia parties, we spent hours talking and getting to know each other. The topics were not superficial; we dove deep into our stories.

"I have a question for you," she said rather seriously on the day after we had first met.

I could see that it was important by the way she was searching my eyes.

"Do you know Jesus?"

I had pushed Him aside for many years. Did I know Jesus? I did know Him. I believed in Him. I had asked Him to come into my life and be my Savior. But I was still angry with Him. I had pushed Him aside for these past few years because I still couldn't understand how He allowed the horrible abuse to happen to me. Where was He? Why didn't He stop it? Why didn't He protect me?

"I know Jesus," I replied. "But I'm angry with God." It was the best, most honest answer I could give her.

She seemed relieved and inquisitive at the same time. But she didn't pry. She nodded, and we moved on to other topics.

Later that night at dinner, as we were still deep in one conversation after another, she looked at me and said, "Why are you angry at God?"

I don't know why, other than I felt secure with this woman. I trusted her. On a deep level, I knew that she was going to be a part of my life. It had been less than forty-eight hours since we met, but I felt safe enough to tell her the deepest, darkest, most hurtful truth of my life. I shared with her about the sexual abuse I had gone through, how I thought God would have protected me and He didn't, and how Kenny had used God as part of his manipulation of me.

I couldn't believe that these words were pouring out of my mouth. But for some reason, my fears about other people finding out, judging me, and thinking of me differently—I didn't have those with her. There was a calmness and safety to her that I had never known in another human being.

She listened carefully, and I could see the sadness on her face and the tears in her eyes for what I had gone through. She thanked me for sharing this story and for being vulnerable and honest with her. Then she just sat with me, holding that safe space to feel what I was feeling, without trying to fix or change anything.

That moment was huge. Not only had I found the woman who I believed was my person, even though it had been such a short time, but she now knew my story, and instead of rejecting me or disbelieving me, she cared for me even more. That response was a gift from God. My true healing journey was about to begin.

"HE'S THE ONE"

Diana's Perspective

"You rock like Fraggle Rock."

I typically didn't respond to messages from guys I didn't know on Myspace. But this one made me laugh out loud, so I replied with the lyrics from the Fraggle Rock *theme song. "Cast your cares away . . . worries for another day!"*[5]

This was how I met Micah, or as I knew him then, "Hitch." That was his name on the Myspace social media platform, so I just thought of him as "that Hitch guy."

Micah and I wrote to each other here and there. It was never "Hey baby" talk, but always respectful and just to see what the other was up to, as we were in the same fitness space.

I lived in San Antonio at the time, was single, and enjoyed our brief conversations.

I lived next to a track, and in the summer of 2008, Muscle & Fitness *magazine published an article about sprinting. I took my copy over to the track and tried out several of the sprint workouts. They kicked my butt, so I kept that issue of* M&F *on top of my enormous stack of fitness magazines so I could do them again.*

Sometime within the next couple of days, I got a message from "Micah." Micah? Who is Micah? I thought. The message sounded like it was from "Hitch," but the name had changed. I clicked through to his profile page. I'll admit, I had never actually done that before, so I hadn't seen many pictures of him other than the little profile image that showed up in his messages.

It was *that "Hitch" guy! I guess his real name is Micah. But that wasn't what grabbed my attention. My jaw dropped when I started scanning his profile. What did I see? It was the sprinting article from* Muscle & Fitness. *And Micah was the model in the article! What? You've got to be kidding me, I thought. I was out there doing those workouts and didn't even realize it was him!*

I wrote to let him know and congratulated him on the feature.

We continued chatting back and forth and struck up a friendship. We even spoke on the phone one night and discovered that we both had a deep passion for helping people and teaching them how to take charge of their health and fitness.

The Olympia weekend in Las Vegas was coming up. I typically went to the expo on my own, met up with friends, and did a lot of networking. It was always a productive time. I reached out to Micah to see if he would be there, and if so, that we should meet up and take a picture.

He was, and we agreed to text and find each other at the expo to grab that photo together.

Wow, his teeth are so white!

That was my thought when I saw Micah for the first time. He saw me and gave me a big smile, teeth just gleaming. He had tanned skin and, of course, was in great shape and was rocking a black tank top. Our connection was instant. It felt like we had been friends forever. I was attracted to him, but this was something more.

At this time in my life, I had been single for quite a while. After running away from the Lord for nearly a decade, I was starting to build a relationship with Him. As a result, I had committed to the Lord that I would never date anyone outside my faith again. I had tried this in the past, and it always failed. It was a dealbreaker for me if someone didn't already know Jesus as their personal Savior. I wasn't going to date with the hopes of changing or converting someone; I wouldn't invest in a romantic relationship unless we already shared that foundation.

I knew I would have to bring the topic of faith up sooner rather than later. I didn't want to waste my time or his, and I didn't want to develop any deeper feelings than I already had if the answer was no.

It wasn't easy asking Micah if he had a relationship with Jesus—that was a pretty big question for Las Vegas! I remember holding my breath for a second, waiting for his response. This could be the end of it.

I appreciated his honesty when he admitted to being angry with God. I looked into his eyes and saw there was pain. I didn't ask questions; the time wasn't right. I just thanked him for being honest with me.

Micah and I spent as much time as we could together that weekend. We went on our first "date," where he gave me $5 to play one of the slot machines. I ended up winning $80 and giving him his $5 back. That seemed fair to me; he thought it was hilarious.

We sat for dinner and dove right into deep topics. What was this pain that I saw? Why was he angry with God?

As Micah shared the story of his abuse and how his abuser had used God to manipulate him, it broke my heart.

I thanked him for sharing and told him how sorry I was that he had gone through that. I could understand why he was angry at God. We sat there for a long time, talking about so many things. I was amazed at his strength in sharing this pain, something most men would hold inside and not share with another soul. I was devastated that he had gone through this trauma, but I knew instantly that there was something special here.

By the end of the Olympia, we both knew this was it. I had found my person. It was unexpected. Las Vegas and Myspace were the last places I thought I would find the love of my life. But God had a plan, and I knew that my life would never be the same after that weekend.

16
KANSAS CITY

When you know, you know.
   And I knew.

Within two months of meeting Diana, she moved to Kansas City. Neither of us had much money, so she sold her car and rented a U-Haul van to pack up a few belongings and drive from Texas.

We lived in an attic at a friend's house. It was within walking distance of the gym where I trained clients, and Diana planned to start building her own clientele as well.

I shared my concept of Hitch Fit with Diana, and she loved the idea; I was ecstatic because now it wouldn't be just me. We could build it together, and she would be the female voice and face, allowing us to relate to a broader client base.

Our roommate loaned us a few thousand dollars to build a website where we could sell online personal training plans to clients worldwide. We had a book (yes, an actual hard copy book) and a DVD (yes, an actual hard copy DVD) that we would mail to each client so that they could read more about living a healthy lifestyle *and* so they would know how to do the exercises that were on the customized plan we would create for them. Then, they would communicate with us via email throughout the entire process, allowing us to track their changes and assist them in overcoming any obstacles along the way.

"What is online personal training?"

I can't even tell you how many times we got that question! This was 2009 and we were some of the originals in the online fitness space, so it was such a foreign concept to people to think that we could work with them as their personal trainer, even if they didn't come into the gym. The idea that they could have a plan which included nutrition guidance and their workouts and support from us, that they could follow along with and check in, and achieve the same solid results as a client who came into Hitch Fit Gym seemed outlandish. But it worked! When we had clients who did an incredible job, whom we had never even met in person, and only ever communicated with online, yet they lost twenty pounds, fifty pounds, seventy-five pounds or more—people were blown away. More clients, from around the globe, started to sign up and join Hitch Fit. It was an exciting time and we were growing fast.

Owning our gym was a dream for both of us. When the opportunity came to take over the space we were training clients out of and turn it into the first official Hitch Fit Gym, we jumped at the chance.

We still had little cash, but we were saving and working hard. We also had debt we were aggressively paying off.

We had to move fast because the former renter had given very little notice, and we would have to flip the gym over the weekend so we could start training our clients there.

"We are going to need $12,500," I told Diana.

That's how much I had calculated: We would need to buy some mats, a rack of dumbbells, a used piece of cardio equipment, a couple of used machines I had found on Craigslist, some paint, and some signage.

Where are we going to get that money? we both wondered.

But God showed up for us in no time.

I was chatting with one of my clients, letting him know what was happening.

"Do you need money?" he asked.

"We do, actually."

"How much?"

"We need $12,500 to get things started," I replied.

"What if I bought $12,500 worth of training sessions and just sent it to your PayPal? Then you can pay me back with sessions."

My eyes lit up. I couldn't believe this. Yes! That would be amazing.

By the end of the day, we had $12,500 in our account.

Over that weekend, Diana and I were on a mission. We had to get the gym up and running quickly because we had clients who wanted to train, and we couldn't afford to keep them waiting.

We bought paint, both white and a bright "Hitch Fit" blue for the walls. We scoured Craigslist and found a bunch of used equipment that would do the trick. An old cable machine, a dumbbell rack, a leg press, Smith machine, leg extension, an elliptical, a bike, and a couple of benches. We added some bands, balls, and smaller equipment that Diana had brought with her from Texas, and *voilà*! Hitch Fit was ready to rock!

By the end of the weekend, with the help from a couple of our one-on-one clients who had trucks and wanted to help and do anything they could to get us up and running, we had assembled our bare-minimum gym, painted the walls, cleaned the bathrooms, picked up supplies like toilet paper and soap from The Dollar Store, and, most importantly, set up the stereo system and a mini "transformation wall" showcasing the before-and-after pictures of a couple of our clients.

It wasn't fancy, but it was ours. We were so energized, and the excitement was contagious. When our first clients showed up on Monday, we were so proud to show them our new space. We didn't need a lot of equipment to help people transform, which became evident quickly. Clients following our system started transforming, and the word of Hitch Fit spread through the city. We knew that we were going to change a lot of lives in this space. It felt amazing to be able to help people using the same methods that had helped me so much.

My dream was coming to life. I could hardly believe it. Diana and I spent every moment together, discovering that was what we preferred. We had to learn how to communicate and work through the challenges that came up. We had different styles initially. Diana was more used to keeping things inside if she was upset, but because of all I had been through, I wanted to tackle things head-on and resolve them as quickly as possible. She learned that she liked my style; she had never been with anyone who got her to communicate and express her feelings. For us, this was working.

We set solid boundaries around our relationship, and it was something that we just did naturally. We didn't have a conversation about it. Being so visible in the fitness world, we both understood how important that protection was around what we had. When it came to phones and computers, we freely had access to each other's, we shared passwords, both of us just wanting to build solid trust in each other, and we highly valued loyalty. If either of us received inappropriate messages from someone on social media, anything that we would deem disrespectful to our relationship, we would block those people. We didn't want to open any doors to things that could disrupt the loving relationship that we were building and growing together. Since she already knew my darkest secrets, I didn't feel like I had to hide from her. We had a foundational safety in our relationship, and we knew that even when we had disagreements, which weren't frequent to begin with, neither of us was going anywhere. We were on each other's team, no matter what.

Thinking about those days brings a smile to my face. We didn't have much money, but we had each other and a dream. We were happy. Building and growing something together with a woman I trusted and loved made me feel safer and more secure than ever.

I knew Diana was a gift from God. The gratitude I felt for her and for what God was doing in all aspects of my life was one reason I started to turn my eyes back to Him. We were married in 2011, and I began to see the love that Diana poured out on me as my wife as a reflection and proof of God's love for me.

Diana was hungry to grow closer to the Lord, and not just on her own; she wanted us to grow together and get to know who He really was. I realized I wanted that too. Instead of running away and being angry and blaming God for what happened to me, I started to see that His heart grieved and was broken for what I had gone through. I began to understand that what Kenny did to me was pure evil. As I started getting to know the Lord better, I saw He loved me so much and wanted to help me heal. I became more hopeful that this was possible. I started to believe that there was freedom from the trauma of my past. It would take work to get there, but I sensed that God would give me the strength I needed.

We felt that the Lord had so much more for us under the marriage covenant, and we couldn't wait to continue stepping into all He had in store for us. We both wanted to help people transform, but beyond the weight loss, we wanted them to heal on even deeper levels. Little did we know how tough that was going to turn out to be at times, how much more pain we would have to work through, or how big this mission would end up being.

17

THE FIGHTING CYCLE

"Micah, why have you always been so mad at me? I didn't do anything to you. I gave you everything. You were a bad kid. You never appreciated all I did for you."

The fights with my mother always seemed to go in a circle. Even years later, the arguing continued without end. The strange thing was that we constantly argued about the same events that had happened well over twenty years earlier. There was no progression in the conversation. Our relationship was stuck in time, back in the years of my abuse.

It drove Diana crazy. There weren't many negatives in our life together, but when I accepted a phone call from my mother, and hours later we were having the same conversation and fighting over and over about things from the past, Diana would finally get frustrated, look at me, and say, "Hang up the phone!"

Though so much was going amazing in my life, my relationship with my mother steadily declined as I got older. I realize now that I had a lot of anger, hurt, and resentment. I had felt abandoned so many times. I felt like I wasn't protected, and those feelings gnawed at me.

But having a natural, lucid conversation wasn't a possibility. Anytime I tried to share with her how I felt about those years of abuse, she was always the victim. She wasn't to blame for anything that happened to me. She even told me that since I chose to go back to the home of a predator, it was my fault. I must have wanted to be abused. I must have liked it.

These conversations triggered me in ways I didn't realize. My mind would go into a frenzy as I was always thrown back into a state of fight or flight. In an instant, I was that little boy, feeling helpless, weak, and confused. It would take me hours and sometimes days to return to a balanced place mentally after a conversation with my mother.

It was hard for me to hear her say hurtful things and to be strong enough mentally not to receive them or believe them. Diana helped immensely in this regard. When my mother told me that I was a bad son, that any money I sent her was not enough, that I was selfish and even "the son of the devil," it made me question if she was right. Maybe I was worthless after all. Diana would always be there, turning my mind back to the truth. My mother was a hurt person, and hurt people hurt people. The way she knew best to deal with her unresolved pain was by trying to manipulate me, and she would do it any way she thought would work.

"You're not conversing with someone who is rational-thinking or who is mentally well," Diana would say, trying her best to encourage and validate me. "You can't take anything that she says to heart. It's not true, and you can't let it control you. We have to pray for her. She's not well."

But my wife was getting fed up.

I was so worked up after a call with my mother that it would cause arguments between Diana and me. It was one of the only things that we argued over. I was so emotionally charged and triggered after the calls that my thinking was erratic and impulsive. One conversation would leave me reeling and upset for days.

I love my mother. Though I don't have a relationship with her, I love her. I believe she went through abuse and trauma that she never did the healing work for, and I know now that unresolved trauma can wreak havoc on your life in so many ways, including decision-making and relationships. Being on the other side of an immense healing journey myself, it makes me sad that she remains stuck.

"This has to stop," Diana said one day. "This relationship is toxic. There is no need to talk about nonsense repeatedly on the phone for hours. It's pointless. It turns you into a different person. You need to establish boundaries so this chaos doesn't control you."

I knew she was right. I had to set clear boundaries with my mother if I was going to stay mentally healthy and balanced. So I stopped taking her calls and limited our contact to texting.

It worked, sort of. Just because I didn't answer the phone didn't mean she wouldn't call and leave message after message. Sometimes, they would start nice. Sometimes she would say, "I love you," and then other times, they turned ugly: that she hated me, that I was abusing her. The thing that got me the most fired up was when she would start talking bad about Diana. In some of her messages, her words would slur, and sometimes it seemed like she would pass out for several minutes before waking back up and continuing to tell me what an awful son I was.

My mother chose victimhood and still does. But I still have hope for her, just like anyone else who has gone through trauma and hasn't undergone healing. Sometimes, staying the victim is just easier than doing the work to be the victor in your life. This was devastating to witness throughout my life. But at the same time, it motivated me.

I refused to stay stuck in the past. I was not going to live in a place of hate. I was going to do the work to heal. I am not a victim. I'm not just a survivor. I'm an overcomer.

"SILENCE WON'T WIN"

Diana's Perspective

When I met Micah, I thought he had a close bond with his mother. He'd painted a rosy picture of their relationship, so when I moved to Kansas City and saw it firsthand, it confused me. I soon realized that the story he'd created in his mind was a shield for his heart, to protect himself from the reality of the situation.

Whenever Micah got off the phone with his mom, after a minimum of two hours of cyclical arguments, he looked like a wounded animal. I hated seeing this strong man of mine reduced to a fragile little boy from a mental and emotional perspective. It would take him a couple of days to return to his normal, happy self.

I wanted to help, but to be honest, I didn't quite know how. I felt relief when he agreed to stop taking calls and keep the contact to text messages only.

Her letters started arriving shortly after that, pages and pages long, front and back, all handwritten. The words were like razor blades. They cut him straight to the heart.

The letters reopened wounds of doubt, shame, and fear of what others might think if he were to speak the truth. I watched Micah wrestle with their weight, his spirit shaken, questioning himself, wondering if the biting words were true. It devastated me to see the impact they had on him. We were working hard to build our life and business together, so many wonderful things were happening, so I decided to take action. I would not let those words steal our joy.

To protect him, I would take the letters and read them first, acting as a shield. It brought a sense of relief to Micah instantly. If there were any messages of kindness, I shared them with him. If they were filled with words intended to wound, I blocked those darts from reaching his tender heart.

> *I saw Satan's hand in those words, trying to keep Micah silent, to trap him in the lie that he was less than the man God made him. Even though the letters keep coming, by God's grace, they no longer have an impact. It's amazing to see how something that once could cause so much pain no longer holds any power.*

18
WORLD CHAMPION

"And the first-ever WBFF Muscle Model Pro World Champion is... Micah LaCerte!"

A *world champion*. From "Chicken Legs" to 2011 Muscle Model World Champion.

I stood on the stage, gratefully accepting my trophy, congratulating my fellow competitors, and thanking the Lord for this achievement.

I was never originally interested in competing in fitness and bodybuilding shows. I loved being a fitness model and working with magazines, and I was content to continue in that lane. But Diana loved competing. It was how she got her start in fitness. Preparing for the stage had given her the motivation she needed to go through her own fitness transformation, losing over fifty pounds and then going on to become a two-time world champion. (Yes, I outkicked my coverage when I married this woman!)

Because it was important to her, and she wanted me to join her, I competed for the first time in 2009, landing my Pro status with the WBFF organization. I didn't love the stage, but doing these shows opened the door to many new opportunities and relationships, and it was also beneficial for business and the growth of Hitch Fit. In 2011, during my third competition, I worked and trained harder than ever to achieve my best physical condition to date. I was ready; I knew I was at my best, and hearing my name called the World Champ, I was beyond grateful.

I was also ready to be done. That would be my last competition, as I would like to be able to say "I went out as a champion!"

When Diana and I reconvened after the show (she took second place that year in the Pro Fitness Model division), I couldn't help but reflect on how far I had come and how fitness, and now my faith, had truly turned my life around.

It was time to start tackling more serious goals. The fitness accolades were amazing, but something stirred in my heart, telling me that there was more and that it was time to start digging deep and doing the work to get to where God needed me to be.

19
FOR SUCH A TIME AS THIS

Lucia wept.

Uncontrollable sobs shook her body as she released mountains of pain, shame, and guilt that were shoved in the deepest part of her soul.

She sat in the small office of Hitch Fit Gym in Kansas City and poured her heart out, sharing her gut-wrenching truth.

For years, she had endured severe sexual abuse. To make herself invisible, she ate. To make her body as unattractive as possible, she gorged herself on junk food. It wreaked havoc on her health. Now she was morbidly obese, diabetic, with high blood pressure and sky-high cholesterol, and not a shred of confidence or belief in herself. She could barely move her body and couldn't look another person in the eye.

But she had a daughter and a son.

She didn't want to die.

She needed to do something.

And she knew she couldn't do it alone.

Praying desperately for solutions, she ended up here, at this gym, sitting in an office with me. She shared with me, a man, something she had never revealed to another person in her entire life, sensing I was who God had sent to help her.

I held my breath for a moment as I fought back tears and the lump rising in my throat.

I prayed silently for the right words to speak. Her pain was palpable. I could understand every emotion: the shame, the guilt, the blame, wondering if it was her fault, if she deserved it, worried that others would find out and judge her, and, at times, wondering if she should take her life and end it all.

I felt every word. I knew this place of deep pain, heartache, darkness, and fear. I knew it because I had been there. Lucia didn't know why God led her into this office, but I knew. My pain had a purpose. Because of what I had gone through, I could relate to her, and I knew I could help her on this healing journey. It was about so much more than losing a number on the scale.

"For such a time as this, my son, for such a time as this," I felt a whisper from the Lord in my spirit, and I understood the assignment. My pain and struggle were the exact reasons that I was going to be able to help Lucia in her time of need. In that moment, I had a strange sensation and realized it was gratitude. I was grateful, not for the abuse I had gone through, but that I had endured pain and could relate. I was thankful that I could understand and help Lucia walk through the pain that kept her in chains.

I gently reached my hand out to Lucia, and as she reached back and clutched it, I said, "It's time to heal, Lucia. You're going to get through this, and God sent me to help. It's going to be you, me, and Jesus, and we will get through this to a healthy place."

When Lucia left the gym that day, you could see the hope in her eyes. Every day after that, when she showed up for her workouts, that hope began to rise. Diana noticed it too. At first, Lucia would avoid all eye contact, but as she recognized that this was a safe space for her, she started to look up.

Hitch Fit was more than a gym; it was becoming a place for healing to happen. As I got a taste of what it was like to help people transform on the deepest levels, it became addictive. I wanted more, and more is what God sent.

20
TRANSFORMING LIVES

"Hitch Fit is Kansas City's number one place for body transformations . . . yeah!"

Diana and I walked around the house and the gym singing our own little Hitch Fit jingle so often that we decided to have a musician turn it into a song that we used in one of our television commercials, which aired throughout the city.

And what that song testified to was the truth: Hitch Fit had become not only the leading gym for transformations in Kansas City but also one of the nation's top transformation training gyms. We wanted to help people transform, we stayed in our lane, and that intense focus enabled us to be the best in the business.

People saw the remarkable stories and transformation photos through our marketing, which enticed them to explore either our gyms or our online training and embark on a fitness journey with us.

But the truth was that the pictures, what people saw happen on the outside, were just the icing on the cake. Coaching people through transformation meant so much more to us than simply helping them change their bodies. That part feels great, of course, but it's what happens on the inside that drives me and has the most significant impact on these people's lives.

I've helped thousands of men and women transform. Some I've worked with for just a few months; others have been in my life for years, allowing me to navigate the ups and downs alongside them. I believe that you can only help someone transform as far as you've gone yourself, from the inside out. I could teach anyone how to eat and exercise to get their body to change; that part was easy. But teaching them how to dig deeper and tackle some of the bigger wounds, encourage them to heal, break free from guilt and shame, and move toward freedom in their lives—now *that* is transformation that I know isn't something every coach can do, but I can.

Two stories of men I had the chance to work with stand out for different reasons, and I asked them, Ben and Rob, to share what their journey with me was like. Each of them had amazing before-and-after photos that wowed people, leading many others to try Hitch Fit. But each faced his unique battles and claimed major victories that the pictures can't capture. Both of these men carried hidden pain that was causing damage mentally and wreaking havoc physically. From day one, I saw potential in them that they didn't see, and I was determined to help them break free and charge toward it.

"BREAKING THROUGH THE SUFFERING"

Ben's Story

I didn't expect the conversation that would change my life to begin in the back of a distillery.

It was the Big Brothers Big Sisters Most Wanted Auction—one of the largest events I had ever attended, filled with Kansas City's brightest, most driven leaders. And yet, in the middle of all that movement and celebration, I was quietly battling insomnia, anxiety, and the feeling that I was failing to be the man I was meant to be.

I spotted Micah at the back of Tom's Town, seated quietly, relaxed, at peace, and yet fully present. There was something different about him. His presence was calm, his energy sincere. It was more than charisma or confidence; it was his spirit. He moved with the type of integrity and humility that made me feel safe. I didn't hesitate. I walked straight to him, introduced myself, and asked if we could talk.

Micah and I dove into a conversation that covered everything I had been carrying silently: faith, fitness, fatherhood, marriage, manhood. I had been pushing through life, raising kids, holding things together, trying to be strong, but inside I was exhausted. I didn't feel like the best version of myself. I was tired of hiding it, tired of hurting quietly. I didn't want pity or a handout—I wanted purpose. And in that conversation, God showed me that Micah might be the guide to help me find it.

I spilled my heart and my fears, my questions about manhood, faith, purpose, and fitness. Micah didn't flinch. He listened. We talked about next steps, and shortly after, I signed up for personal training at Hitch Fit. On the surface, I told myself I was there to lose weight and drop the "dad bod." But I quickly realized God had signed me up for far more than physical change. God had bigger plans than just fitness. What began as a physical transformation quickly became a spiritual and emotional rebuilding.

The first workout wrecked me. I threw up after that session. It was like walking into a buffet thinking I could handle everything on the menu—and realizing I was full after just a few bites. My mind was motivated, but my body had to catch up. So I kept showing up. After about six weeks, I started seeing real change. The pounds came off, but even more, the weight within started lifting.

Micah's workouts came with wisdom. Every rep was therapy. Every session was a spiritual check-in. I found myself opening up in ways I never had. We'd talk about life, fatherhood, trauma, legacy. Sometimes we ended sessions in prayer, other times in silence, just taking in what God was doing. What stood out most was Micah's ability to be both grounded and vulnerable, unafraid to talk about his past, yet unwavering in his commitment to the present. His consistency was unmatched. And it inspired me to take my life seriously and become a better man.

I dropped from 188 pounds to 159 and hit 6 percent body fat in just ninety days. But more than that, I found purpose again. I had more energy with my kids, two sons and a daughter, and I was finally able to be present. I wasn't too tired to play or too distracted to laugh. I could outjump them on the trampoline and still tuck them in with joy. I found myself opening up to others, sharing what I had kept inside for years, hoping that my story could spark change for someone else, especially men in my community who suffer in silence.

I learned that strength isn't just physical. It's emotional. It's spiritual. It's choosing to lean on God when your own understanding fails. It's recognizing that sometimes you have to walk away from toxic people, places, and patterns to step into who God designed you to be.

If you watched my transformation, you would've seen the smile come back. You would've seen a broken man become whole again, not because of dumbbells or diet plans but because of discipline, prayer, and the presence of a friend who chose to lead with love and purpose.

I entered Hitch Fit broken. I walked out fortified, a man of God, armed with clarity, strength, and vision. And now, I fight my battles with peace in my spirit and purpose in my steps. Maximized in manhood and playing a bigger game.

Ben was ready to do the work, and I mean more than the push-ups and squats. He was ready to do the heavy lifting to get out from under the weight that had been crushing him for so long, and boy, was it worth it. He came in as a client and left Hitch Fit as a brother because we went through the muck together. He didn't back down, and as a result, he saw the ripple effects of healing that had a far greater impact than his newly ripped abs. He broke through the silence that had held him back and started using his story to spark change in those around him. His journey is a shining example of what's possible when you face pain head-on, turning it into a source of strength.

I saw the same potential to turn things around in Rob. His story started quite differently: He came to Hitch Fit after a near-stroke that could have ended his life and a food addiction that was eating him alive. I knew brutal honesty was the only way to break through to a guy like Rob, because sitting across from him on that first day in my office, I saw a man capable of so much more, and I was determined to push him toward it and see if he was willing to put the work in.

Spoiler alert: He was.

"BREAKING POINT TO BREAKTHROUGH"

Rob's Story

In February 2017, while on vacation in Mexico, I suffered a high blood pressure incident. I had been on medication for over a year, but even with that, there were some days my BP was close to 200/100. This was due to terrible eating habits and lack of exercise, even though I'd been working out twice a week with a personal trainer at one of the big-name corporate gyms.

That fateful day in Mexico, I have no idea how high my blood pressure was, but from the symptoms I was having, I'm sure I was on the verge of a stroke. Fortunately, my wife went to the front desk, and one of the concierges ran across the street to a pharmacy and got some medications. Thankfully in Mexico, you don't need a prescription.

My wife, Anissa, decided enough was enough, and while still on vacation, she texted Diana, who she knew from a women's business group in Kansas City, to set us up to do the online version of Hitch Fit. I was reluctant, to say the least. Anissa and I had scheduled a consultation on a Saturday to get things started. I was unable to attend at the last minute due to work, so my wife attended alone. She sat in the office at Hitch Fit Gym with Micah and Diana and broke down. She was sure she would be a widow within a year if something didn't change. Diana encouraged her confidently, "Micah's got this." So she rescheduled my consultation for a couple of days later.

As I drove to Hitch Fit to meet Micah, I wasn't excited about it. It was raining hard, and I had difficulty finding a parking place. I took that as a sign I should just go home. But thankfully, I didn't. Now, understand that I had known Micah for several years on a social level, so I wasn't intimidated to meet with him; I just didn't have much interest in making a change in my life! I was extremely complacent in how bad my health was. Well, Micah had a plan to drive that complacency right out of me.

Since I already had some familiarity with Micah, I wasn't shocked or intimidated (much) by his appearance. I knew him to be kind and friendly, despite his Adonis-like appearance. Well, all that changed very quickly when we sat down to talk.

He hit me with a brutal truth. I was the fat, funny guy everybody loved. I was the fat, funny guy who ate too much, drank too much, and, quite frankly, was going to die if I didn't change my behavior. He also told me my wife hadn't signed up for this life and what I was doing was careless and inconsiderate to her. Something to note is that I can experience some bipolar type of anger rages when someone pushes me a little too much. But at this moment, I knew his words were honest and accurate, and they brought me to tears.

I decided rather than an online training plan, I needed to be around Micah on a regular basis. There was something about him that I knew would push me to become a better version of myself. I couldn't quite pinpoint it, but he had a strength beyond his bulging biceps, and I wanted that for myself.

On day one of my transformation journey, Micah put me through a workout that I wasn't sure I'd walk away from, literally! It was brutal. I had never had anyone challenge or push me in that way before. It felt awful and amazing all at the same time. My body was sore, but I felt like I had accomplished something I didn't even think I was capable of. If I could do that, maybe I could do even more?

Micah has a gift, which I later learned is from overcoming his own pain, to push people to their limit, physically, which eventually pushes you mentally and emotionally too. I showed up two days later for my second workout. I was excited, but I feared how hard it would be at the same time. I've got a pretty big ego, though, so before the workout started, I told Micah my transformation would be so great that I'd be one of the giant posters on the wall when it was done—an accomplishment I achieved.

Over the next eight months, I lost over eighty pounds of fat and over fifteen inches off my waistline. It was amazing how I felt. During the process, Micah and I spent hours together sharing stories of challenges we both had faced and pain we'd had to overcome.

Over the next few years, I actively pursued bigger and bigger fitness goals, including getting off many medications, becoming a Hitch Fit Transformation Coach, and even competing in a fitness transformation show (which I won after shedding a whopping 115 pounds!).

Then, in 2019, Anissa and I were asked to step up in a huge way to adopt our two grandchildren, one of whom was nineteen months

> old and the other a newborn. We said yes to this life-changing decision, which, though incredibly challenging, has been an immeasurable blessing.
>
> I know that I wouldn't have been able to accept this massive responsibility if I hadn't gone through the transformation process with Micah. It not only prepared me physically for this huge task, but a great deal of inner healing had taken place, all of which I believe happened because of the healing Micah was also experiencing at that time.
>
> Micah was able to connect with me on a deep level, which truly inspired and motivated me. I'm forever grateful for our relationship and what he helped me accomplish in every way.

It still amazes me that I get the chance to be part of stories like this, and I don't take it lightly. I know what it feels like to be stuck, even if my stuckness looked different from Ben's or Rob's. I understand it, and I know what it takes to get out of the mud and start living a life filled with purpose.

The more I was able to persuade people to believe in themselves, the greater the desire it created in me to help. I got to help people figure out how their toughest pain could turn into their biggest purpose. The Lord was giving me a chance to practice, to dig deep, and to build my transformation muscles, so I could be ready for even more.

21
THE VISION

The ground began to shake
The stone was rolled away
His perfect love could not be overcome
Now death where is your sting
Our resurrected King
Has rendered you defeated
Forever, He is glorified
Forever, He is lifted high
Forever, He is risen
He is alive.[6]

It was March 2017. I sat at the Kari Jobe concert and felt almost as though I was in a trance as she belted out the song "Forever." The words resonated deep into my soul.

At that moment, I closed my eyes, and the Lord gave me two visions, the most vivid visions I've ever had.

Throughout the past few years, Diana and I had been growing our relationship with the Lord and becoming bolder in our faith. I had grown stronger in so many ways, and with the days of fitness competitions behind us, we had both transitioned to helping others with deeper and more meaningful transformations. Hitch Fit was doing well; we had multiple gym locations, and our online business was thriving. Married life suited me. Diana and I were together non-stop, and, as we had discovered, time is both of our primary love languages, so our situation filled both of us up.

I was much more attuned to when the Lord asked something of me, whether it was to speak a word to someone at the gym, pray for someone who was hurting, or give to someone in need. I was no stranger to hearing His voice. But what happened at this concert was unlike anything I had ever experienced.

The first vision was a picture of me going to Haiti with Diana. We were meeting the children at the school that we sponsored there. I saw myself hugging them and holding them. A smile crept over my face, knowing that Diana had wanted me to join her on a trip to Haiti for quite some time, and I knew that now I was supposed to go.

Then, the second vision came flooding in. This one caught me by surprise, and I sucked in my breath sharply as the picture came into focus in my mind.

I was standing on a stage in front of an audience, sharing the story of the abuse that nearly destroyed my life.

My eyes shot open. I looked at Diana, who was in full worship mode and had no clue what I had just experienced.

Lord, I don't know if I can do it. Please don't ask this of me.

Fear swept over me. For a moment, I felt terror and panic at the thought of this mission. My stomach felt nauseous. My heart started racing.

Kari kept singing the powerful words, "You have overcome. You have overcome. You have overcome."

I closed my eyes and breathed deeply. Jesus had overcome, and He would help me overcome. At that moment, the strangest sense of peace settled on me.

I knew God had just shown me something He wanted me to do. It would be my choice to say yes or no. To fulfill this vision, I would need to share and be vulnerable so that He could use my story to help others heal. I wasn't ready yet—that was evident—but I sensed that God was going to provide the breakthroughs that would enable me to lead others to breakthroughs too.

My mind raced for the rest of the concert. I couldn't wait to get to the car to talk to Diana about everything. Even though I didn't know when this vision would become reality, it gave me a sense of purpose. I could help others, and it would be in far greater ways than just with weight loss.

If I were brave enough to say yes to this call from the Lord, could I help thousands? Maybe millions of men and women, just like me, who felt trapped by the pain, shame, and guilt they had gone through? At that moment, I could see others being set free. As I thought this through and envisioned the faces of the people I could help, my fears subsided. What had felt like terror started to feel like anxious anticipation. Maybe even excitement.

Right then I took a deep breath, closed my eyes, and said, "Yes, Lord, I'm all in."

"I had a vision," I blurted out to Diana as soon as we got in the car after the show.

She looked at me expectantly.

"I saw myself in Haiti with the kids. It's time for me to go. And . . . I saw myself on a stage sharing my story."

She just stared at me for a moment. Her mouth dropped open, but nothing came out.

After a long pause, she nodded and said, "Okay."

We both knew it was *go* time.

Visiting Haiti and seeing our children for the first time happened within the year. As Diana and I walked across the field toward the schoolhouse, holding hands, it was just as my vision had unfolded. I could hear the children's voices singing to us as we approached. It was one of the most beautiful and profound moments of my life. To meet them, hug them, play with them, and see the gratitude and joy in their eyes was life-giving.

The second vision was going to take a bit more time. The details weren't clear yet, but I felt like when it was time, I would know.

"Micah, I would like you to consider sharing your testimony at church."

I had entrusted my pastor of the small church we attended with the truth about my past. He had provided me with extensive guidance and mentoring over the past few years. He had helped me deepen my relationship with the Lord and been instrumental in showing me the truth of who Jesus was, as opposed to the warped version of religion and faith that Kenny had immersed me in.

I wasn't sure about sharing with the church at first. But I prayed about it and realized that this would be a safe setting, surrounded by people who loved me, where I could practice what I knew was coming sometime in the future. I said yes.

I rehearsed repeatedly what I would say and how I would say it. I recorded myself. I went on long walks and repeated the words of my speech. Somehow, sifting through those painful memories and compiling them into a timeline story for people to hear and understand helped me process what I'd gone through to an even deeper level. Even though there were times of fear, when I felt stuck thinking about a certain part of my past for too long, I pushed and prayed my way through it, and talked it out with Diana.

I started to see that young, abused version of me from the viewpoint of a heart-involved observer. I started to understand that I was just a child and shouldn't have had to carry that fear, shame, and guilt. The abuse wasn't my fault. I grew such a compassion for my younger self. I saw him. I knew him. Even though he was forever a part of me, I was no longer him. Though I grieved deeply for the loss of his innocence, I was starting to feel great hope for the possibility of transformational healing.

My desire to help others grew immensely through this process. I especially wanted to help men who are going through life in bondage from the pain of their abuse, pretending that everything is fine while they still have not healed and the impacts of that pain are destroying their lives.

The most important thing I wanted to convey was that this wasn't a story about me remaining a victim. This wasn't just about surviving abuse but, through God's grace, thriving on the other side of it. I wanted to show that it was possible to heal from deep wounds. My wounds may have left scars, but they didn't hold me back from living a full, purposeful, and impactful life.

When the moment came to share, I prayed that the Holy Spirit would take over my words. I don't even remember what I said, I just let the words pour out: what had happened to me and how the Lord had sent lifelines to save me through people, fitness, and renewed faith.

I ended with an altar call, inviting anyone who needed prayer for their own healing to come up. When both men and women in the audience left their seats and came forward, I prayed over them.

One woman just came up and hugged me. No words were spoken. She wept. It felt like she was releasing years of pent-up pain in that moment. Another man came up and told me that he almost didn't show up that night. But the Lord had pressed on him heavily that he needed to be there, and now he knew why.

I looked at Diana and could see tears welling up in her eyes. I felt a bit of weight had lifted from me. I was on the journey to my next phase of life, and I knew without a shadow of a doubt that this was the work the Lord was calling me to.

I wasn't alone.

This was one of the greatest revelations to me as I started researching what was out there for men who had gone through childhood sexual abuse. I heard frequently about women who had been abused, but I rarely, if ever, heard about men.

As I started digging in, I realized I was joining an army of other male survivors who found healing as they stepped into their purpose to help others.

Author Gary Roe said of his own experience of abuse, "When my flashbacks began to come, I told God that I wouldn't survive unless the purpose was bigger than myself. I hated the abuse, and I detested the idea that other boys—right now—are being molested by predators. 'I want to become a warrior against abuse,' I told God, and invited him to use me in the war to fight such an insidious evil."[7]

There is power in purpose. And purpose often awaits us on the other side of recovery, as it was for me.

22
THE HOUSE

"It's gone."

I sat in disbelief, staring at the empty lot. It was surrounded by a wire fence, unkempt and immersed with vines and weeds.

Diana stared at me, her eyes wide in amazement, jaw dropped. She didn't say a word but grabbed her camera and started to capture my response to this unbelievable moment.

We were both awestruck. The house was gone.

Diana and I don't give gifts for birthdays or holidays. Instead, we prefer experiences or trips.

For her forty-second birthday, she wanted to travel down the West Coast, visit multiple national parks, and hike and explore our way from Seattle to LA.

Since we were flying into Seattle to launch our adventure, I knew there was something I had to do. I needed to go back to the house where Kenny had mercilessly abused me, night after night. As part of the healing journey I was on, I needed to see it, to face it, and to know that what happened to me there did not define who I was. It no longer had control over me.

If you've gone through something similar, maybe there's some place you need to revisit too. That house, basement, attic, or closet that you were hurt in, that space that holds so much of your pain. Perhaps you need to face it, too, knowing that it doesn't define you and hasn't defeated you.

We landed in the city and picked up the rental car. Seeing the home was the top priority on our list because I knew that until it was over, I wouldn't be able to focus on anything else.

We checked in at our hotel, and I felt anxiety creeping in as we hopped back in the car to make the thirty-minute drive to this address that lived in my dreams as a house of horror.

It was a beautiful day, but my mind raced as we approached. Seeing the sign from the highway with the town's name triggered me.

All those years ago, I felt helpless and hopeless. I didn't know how my life would turn out. I thought I would be damaged goods. I didn't know if I would ever find a safe and loving relationship, something that I longed for when I was young. My life was filled with so much confusion, fear, and pain back then.

As those thoughts flew through my mind, I looked over at Diana, who was quietly gazing out the window at the scenery, and felt a surge of gratitude. I wasn't alone. I had made it through. I wasn't hopeless or helpless any longer.

We arrived at the street and drove up slowly. There was the river I fished in and the basketball court I practiced at for hours. The memories flooded back in. I pointed everything out to Diana. She had heard these stories for so many years, and now being able to show her where everything happened felt surreal.

The home was just around the corner now. I mentally steeled myself to face it. In my mind, I was prepared to wipe that house out and close a dark chapter of my life, releasing the pain that it held over me.

We pulled up. I stopped the car in the middle of the street and stared.

I couldn't believe my eyes.

Diana looked at me curiously.

"What are you doing? Is this it?" she asked.

I looked over at her, my mind swirling with questions too. "It was here. This was it. It was *right here*."

My mind worked to process what I was seeing.

The house was gone.

I stepped out of the car and walked toward that space where so much evil had been done to me. I looked through the fence, letting this truth sink in.

I looked at Diana, silently following me with her video camera as I soaked it all in, waiting for me to share what was going on in my heart.

"God came in and demolished the house. He tore it down. So much bad happened out of that place," I said, choking back the tears, "and God took care of it.

"It allows me to move on, forgive, and release it. I'm so thankful and grateful for what the Lord has done in my life.

"I don't know what to say . . . it's gone, and you can heal. No matter what you go through, if you've got Christ . . ."

That was all I could put into words.

In my heart, I heard the Lord saying to me, "It is finished."

23
COVID

"We've got to close the gyms down for two weeks."

It was March 2020, and Diana and I were glued to the news, trying desperately to make sense of what was going on in our country with the COVID-19 virus. When the mandate came to Kansas City that businesses had to close to stop the virus from spreading, we complied, hopeful that this wouldn't last long.

We were grateful that we had been in the online training business for over a decade; as many other fitness coaches were trying to pivot to figure out online platforms quickly, we already had ours in place. We knew that exercising and eating healthily would be critical for people, not just for the physical benefits but for the boost to the immune system and the mental health impact. We knew that the best thing we could do for ourselves, and others, was to choose faith over fear and to be a source of hope and encouragement daily.

Each day, we worked diligently on what we could do. We went on Facebook live and led people through workouts that they could do at home. We spread messages of health and hope as far and wide as we could, and for me, I knew it was time to start working on a project that the Lord needed me to tackle.

It was time for me to write my story. All fifty thousand words of it. That's what I felt like the Lord was asking me to do. For someone who isn't a big reader or writer, and who has trouble focusing on one thing for long periods of time, this seemed like an immense ask. But I was committed.

One morning shortly after the COVID shutdown began, I headed to Diana's reading and craft room. It's the quietest spot in our house, with big picture windows and bright green walls. It's where Diana goes to read and to create, so I knew it was the perfect spot for me to dig into the pain and start pouring it out.

I sat at the desk for a moment and looked at the keyboard. Where should I start?

I took a deep breath and closed my eyes, bracing for the memories that I wanted to keep locked up in a compartment, but knowing it was time for them to come out. It was time for all of that darkness to be exposed to the light.

Then I just started typing, letting whatever words came to my mind flow onto the pages . . .

> I have spent the last twenty-plus years of my life thinking about the day that I would sit down, write my story, and share it with the world. In all honesty, this has been one of the most difficult processes I have had to go through because sharing my story meant I had to go to the deepest, darkest place of my soul. I will have to allow the trauma I have gone through to resurface. For thirty years of my life I have hidden what happened to me, and for those same thirty years I have worked most every single day trying to find the "fix" to heal this pain inside me. To fully heal I know I have to share and help others now. I know this next chapter of my life will follow God's purpose.

The words kept flowing as the memories flooded in, some that I had forgotten completely. Each day I confined myself to that room and let the tears flow as the pain came rushing back. I wanted to get *all* of it out; I didn't want *any* of it to have control over me any longer. I kept writing and writing, pouring my soul out, and when I felt like I couldn't take it anymore, I would take a break, go work out, and then come back to it. I started to get in a rhythm with writing as the lockdown dragged on.

I kept showing up, day after day, word after painful word. I didn't hold back. When I needed to cry, I cried; when I needed to scream, I screamed. Anything within me that needed to come out, I let it come out. The words were therapeutic. Writing them felt like a release: I was letting them go, releasing them to God, and preparing to release them to the world so that my story could serve a big purpose.

In the end I had wrestled with every memory; recorded every wound, no matter how painful; and written every thought that had flowed through.

I had journaled *fifty thousand words*.

24

PAIN TO PURPOSE

"We're supposed to host a conference."

Diana and I were sitting on the balcony of a resort in Mexico. It was May 2022, and we had just concluded cohosting a fitness retreat that went beautifully. We are bold about our faith, and the retreat morphed into a faith-and-fitness event that was powerful and more meaningful than we could have imagined.

As we sat gazing out at the ocean, praying together and thanking the Lord for such a great time, He gave Diana a glimpse of what was to come.

It was clear as day to her, and if you know my wife, you know that once she has a vision from the Lord, she jumps in and says yes. It's going to happen.

"It will be the stage where you share your story," she continued.

I knew that she was right.

I felt a little twinge of fear in my heart. Those old voices of "what will people think of you when they find out?" tried to push their way into my brain, but because my strength in the Lord had grown so much in the past six years, I knew those voices were not from Him, and I realized there would be resistance in this journey, because the enemy sure didn't want me doing this.

But God was saying, *Go*.

The journey to that stage would be one of the most challenging of our lives, with twists and turns that we never imagined.

"I'm calling to let you know that Travis is dead."

The words took my breath away. It felt like a wrecking ball had just crashed straight through my chest.

The only sound I could manage to get out was a guttural "Noooo."

Diana and I were sitting on the couch at about 8:30 on a Saturday night, February 4, 2023. We were watching a show together and just winding down for the night, about ready to head to bed.

Earlier that day, we were texting back and forth with our friend Travis, who was also our partner in the retreat business. We loved him dearly. He was one of those unicorn human beings who walked into a room and lit it up. He never met a stranger and would be friends with an entire group of people in an instant. He had a big personality, the likes of which Diana and I had never met. The texts from earlier were about big plans for our retreats in the future. There was so much excitement. He signed off as he was heading out to snowmobile with friends in Wyoming, having just celebrated his birthday a couple of days before. We wished him well and to have a great time on the trails.

And that was it.

The last messages that we would ever send or receive.

In an instant, he was gone.

The phone call that night crushed us. We lay on the floor in our living room, sobbing, but knew we had to pull it together and reach out to start letting others know. It was a long, hard night. Neither of us could sleep as we cried out to the Lord, asking *Why?* We were crushed for his wife and children, knowing how unbearable this blow was for them. Things that seemed so certain just a short time before were now total unknowns.

On top of the sadness, we had to switch our minds into business mode. We had a retreat coming up in just five weeks, with nearly ninety people signed up, who all loved Travis and who would be grieving his loss. Additionally, we were locked into contracts for the conference and for additional retreats.

As our heads started to clear from the clouds of grief, we realized that we needed to step up and carry on. We needed to be strong—a strength we knew the Lord would provide—to take on the responsibility for these contracts and commitments, for which the load landed squarely on us.

We surged forward. Diana and I both felt strongly that the Lord had brought Travis into our lives for a purpose, even though it was for a shorter season than we would have liked.

We assumed all the financial and legal responsibilities of existing contracts. We stepped in to host a conference, something we had never done, in Tampa (where Travis had lived), a city where we had no established network.

You know you have a God-sized goal when the only way you will pull it off is if He steps in and does it, which is exactly what He did.

Diana came to me one day and shared something powerful. "You know, the Lord told me that we were to host a conference. I think I said yes to it so quickly because I thought Trav would be with us; my confidence was in him, that he would be able to help in Tampa and get the connections. But the Lord revealed something to me, and it really hit me. He said, *I told you to host a conference, but I didn't tell you Travis would be with you. Your confidence needs to be in* Me *and nothing else."*

That landed hard for her. Her trust needed to be planted on the *one* firm foundation: the Lord. From then on, we both ensured our confidence was in God and Him alone.

The Lord pushed and stretched us through the planning of that event. I was intensely focused on sharing my story. I prayed, practiced, and prayed some more that the Lord would give me the right words.

At the same time, I had put pressure on myself to get my book written in time for the conference. I found a ghostwriter to help me with the composition. I was determined we needed to have this book done by the time I took the stage in January 2024. But midway through the project, I knew it wasn't right. In my heart, I knew the story had to come through Diana. This left me in a bit of a panic, as the conference was in less than three months. How could the book possibly be finished by then?

I shared my thoughts with Diana, and she looked at me helplessly. This was too much to ask right now, but she also knew it was supposed to be her.

Why were we experiencing so much resistance with this project? I knew that God wanted me to share my story, and I was trying to be obedient. Why did everything feel like it wasn't right and that we couldn't complete the assignment?

Over the next couple of weeks, the answer came clearly.

The resistance was from God. He told us to host a conference; He didn't tell us to publish a book before the conference. We were pushing through *our* agenda instead of His.

As soon as I realized that it wasn't His timing, we both had an immense sense of relief. We let it go.

In the meantime, Diana was working day and night, organizing the conference and figuring out countless details, all the while praying that God would send us the right speakers. This went on for months.

The weight seemed unbearable at times. But we knew that the resistance we were up against was because a bigger purpose was at stake. We knew that this was not going to be easy. But we knew that we had to persist, Lean IN to the Lord, and He would help us Level UP. *Lean In Level Up.* There it was: the name of our conference.

We started asking friends in Kansas City if they knew anyone from Tampa. One connection led to another, and another, and another. We met the most incredible people—people we knew were meant to be a part of a bigger picture as we stepped into this new chapter. And through this, the Lord sent us the most incredible lineup of speakers who all said *yes* to being a part of our event, committing their time and their treasure—and many of them barely knew us! We were blown away at how God orchestrated that powerful assembly of incredible humans who would be side by side with us for one of the most meaningful moments of our lives.

We stopped praying for a certain number of people to be in attendance and started praying that the *right* people, who were supposed to be a part of that vision that the Lord had given me nearly seven years before, would be in that room with us. We just surrendered.

Nearly a year with the weight of this massive undertaking on our minds took its toll on Diana. She is so strong, in every way, but the immensity of this step in our lives wasn't lost on her. She poured every ounce of everything she had into creating the most beautiful conference experience possible. She knew the heavy burden that I was feeling as we moved closer and closer to the day when I would stand on that stage and share about the most painful, darkest times of my life.

25
THE "F" WORD

"Do you think you've forgiven Kenny?" Diana asked me curiously.

We were out walking through our neighborhood on a crisp, late fall day in Kansas City. We were both bundled in sweatshirts and moving quickly to stay warm. The pathway was littered with leaves that had fallen, crackling under our feet with every step.

Our four-mile route through the trails in our neighborhood served as a way for Diana and me to connect and discuss what was going on in our world, in our hearts, and in our thoughts. With the conference just a few months away, it was the main topic on most days.

I paused for a moment to think, but before I could answer, she elaborated further on her question.

"I'm asking because you're about to step on a stage and share this story, and I know we talk about forgiveness, and we understand that it's important for freedom, but true forgiveness is from the heart, not just something that you say with words. So I just wonder, Where is your heart with this?"

She wasn't looking for me to give her the "right" answer; she was looking for the *real* answer.

For many years, "forgive" may as well have been a four-letter word as it related to my abuse. What I went through was evil. There's no way I would forgive Kenny for what he did to me. I didn't know if I could forgive my mother for abandoning me. I wasn't even sure if I could forgive myself for the guilt I felt when I discovered Kenny was abusing his sons, thinking there was something I could have done to prevent it.

That was me for decades. It's the norm for abuse survivors, and rightfully so. Initially, I thought forgiving Kenny would mean that I was okay with what he did to me and all of the other kids. I had even heard somewhere that when you forgive, you need to let the person back into your life. Well, no way was that happening (and thankfully, I later learned the truth that forgiving an abuser doesn't mean you ever have to let them into your life again). For years I clung to that unforgiveness and the bitterness it carried. It was mine, and I had every right to hang on to it for dear life. But somewhere along my messy healing journey, as my relationship with the Lord deepened, I started to loosen my white-knuckle grip on it, and I had a breakthrough.

I can't think of an exact moment that I forgave in my heart, but I realized that it had happened one day when I was practicing my speech for the conference. When I got to one of the ugliest parts, one of the moments when Kenny was abusing me, I realized that the disgust and hatred I had felt for him in the past when I recounted this moment were gone. It wasn't that the horror of the moment had changed, but the hatred and anger in my heart about him had changed.

I wasn't triggered by the thought of him or by hearing his name. I felt at peace about it. I knew I had forgiven because I had released Kenny's power over me. I even felt bad for him. As the weight of my traumatic past had lifted from me little by little over the years of healing, I recognized that Kenny was a broken and weak man who lived in bondage to his sin. He desperately needed to come to repentance for what he had done, and I recognized that I genuinely hoped that he would.

I thought through all these things as Diana waited expectantly for an answer.

"I believe I have," I said. "I don't hate him. I hate what he did, but I don't hate him anymore. I feel sad for him. But I know I've forgiven because I've released him and what he did to me; they don't have power over me anymore. I don't think I could share the story without having forgiven him, honestly, because if I were still stuck in that pain and bitterness, I'd still be in bondage. But I'm not. I'm free, and I have a story of freedom to share, and that's exactly what I plan on doing."

That was the real answer. It felt good to say it out loud for the first time.

Diana nodded, satisfied, and switched the conversation to a lighter topic.

I took a deep breath of the cool air and felt refreshed. Something that I once thought was impossible was possible with God. I was ready now, more than ever, to share this story and help others feel this freedom too.

26
LEAN IN LEVEL UP

"Micah has prepared for the last seven years for this moment." Diana choked back tears as she stood on the Lean In Level Up stage in January 2024.

"You are the exact people that God wanted in this room, to be a part of this moment. Thank you for being part of this big step." Her voice was almost in a whisper as the emotion swept over her and the entire room.

Kari Jobe's song "Forever" played softly in the background as Diana prayed and invited the Holy Spirit in. I felt the presence of the Lord, and tears welled up in my eyes, as my strong and beautiful wife introduced me to the stage.

"I was bigger now, I was stronger now . . . surely it wouldn't happen again." The words flowed out of my mouth. I wasn't afraid. God had equipped me for exactly this moment, in this room, with these people.

Over the next hour, as I shared the gut-wrenching details, I could feel more of the burden I had carried for years lifting off of me. The words kept coming, weaving through the tragedy and trauma-shattered pieces of my life, ultimately fighting my way to triumph.

I finished the story by sharing the video Diana had taken of me when we visited the home in Washington and found it demolished. The immensity of this sign of victory was not lost on the crowd.

Every person in that room came down into the depths and then rose up from the ashes with me.

I walked off that stage a new man, a stronger man.

The challenge of publicly sharing my story was like a massive weight. Over the seven years of preparation, I had to build the spiritual, emotional, and mental muscle to push that weight. Every rep counted. When it came time to do that heavy lift, God had equipped me with the strength to do it.

And what's more amazing is that pushing that weight made me even stronger.

Psalm 84:7 says, "They go from strength to strength, till each appears before God in Zion."[8]

Reading this, I see that's what has happened throughout my life. Every situation I went through made me stronger for the next challenge I would face. If it weren't for having to face a prior challenge, I wouldn't have been equipped for what was to come. I had to build the strength, little by little, to become strong in body, mind, and spirit.

I had to fight many battles to become the warrior I know God created me to be. Every battle was a training ground for the bigger plans and purposes ahead.

"THE SPEECH"

Diana's Perspective

My eyes were glued to Micah as he stood on stage. This amazing moment had finally arrived. Few men have the guts to do what

Micah was stepping up for. I have seen him wrestle with the pain his abuse caused as though it was a lion. Sometimes the lion pinned him down, but he'd shake it off and charge back till he won.

I held my breath as his vulnerable words poured out. I remember days when facing those memories hurt so bad he'd freeze, trapped in the past.

I glanced around the room. Every heart was captivated. I saw tears in the eyes of many, including some of the strongest men in the room. I saw the amazement on people's faces as they heard the story unfold. Never in a million years would they have thought Micah had gone through this. The power of his testimony was like a wrecking ball, tearing down walls of fear and shame in one brutal swing.

I've seen my husband do a lot of strong, manly things over the years. He's done tough stuff—lifting weights, building a business—but this topped it all. Men fear that sharing abuse will make them weak. I believe Micah's courage shatters that lie.

My husband is going to change lives, far more than he has thus far, and I can't wait to witness it.

He stepped off the stage into a wave of hugs. Multiple people in that room approached him later to tell him they had gone through something similar. That's the power of testimony.

Coming off the conference, I was on such a spiritual high. This was the greatest level of freedom I had felt in my entire life. The burden I had been carrying for thirty years was now completely lifted. Every ounce of it. *Gone.*

This breakthrough opened the gate for me to help others transform on even deeper levels. The work I was doing through Hitch Fit and now through SoulFIT (our faith-and-fitness-based retreats and conferences business) was more meaningful to me than ever. As you know, I believe a coach can take people only as far as you've gone yourself, and this applies to healing too. I now understood how hard a healing journey can be, regardless of the wound's origin, and since I had traveled the path myself, I was capable of leading others.

The conference not only broke chains for me but also opened the door to new relationships. Every person who shared that sacred space holds a special place in my heart. God placed each of them there for a reason. For some, it was to receive a word of encouragement or a moment of strengthening; for others, the Lord knew it was their time to start a transformation journey, and I would have the honor of being their guide. One of the men that God planted in the room for just that purpose was Ricardo (Ricky) Verduzco, who became a client, a friend, and a trusted brother.

> ## "FROM ROCK BOTTOM TO REAL SUCCESS"
>
> ### Ricky's Story
>
> *When I first met Micah at the Lean In Level Up Conference, I was clawing my way out of the lowest point in my life. I was battling addiction. Drugs, alcohol, and food had become my coping mechanisms. I was spiraling. My marriage was hanging by a thread, my kids were slipping away emotionally, and the business I'd poured years into was on the verge of collapse. I was behind on everything, including the mortgage, car loans, and credit cards. The walls were closing in.*
>
> *About a year before crossing paths with Micah, I decided to pour everything I had into rebuilding the business. It was the only thing I felt I could control. I thought financial stability would be the answer, so I pursued it relentlessly, by any means necessary. In doing*

so, I ignored everything else: my health, my family, my friendships, even myself.

Miraculously, I rebuilt the business to a valuation of $12 million within a year. But at what cost? I was almost 300 pounds, drinking heavily, and deeply unhappy. I wore the mask of success, but inside, I was deteriorating. My health was failing, my marriage was strained, and my relationship with my kids was nearly nonexistent. All I knew was work, and nothing else seemed to matter.

Then, I attended the SoulFIT conference in Tampa. I sat in the audience and listened to Micah share his story. I was blown away by his vulnerability around his trauma, the strength he had built through transformation, and the boldness of truth that he shared that day. It hit me like a lightning bolt. I didn't just hear him; I felt him. And I knew I needed to speak with him.

When we first spoke, all I could talk about was business. That was my identity. But even in that shallow exchange, I sensed something deeper pulling at me. I didn't know exactly what it was, but I knew I needed to work with Micah on a personal level. He had something that I desperately craved. There was a confidence about him that wasn't rooted in business success, though I knew he had that. There was a peace about him beyond how much money he had in the bank or how fit his body was. I was intrigued and knew that this was someone I wanted in my circle; I wanted what he had.

I found out Micah had an Inner Circle program where he worked with men like me for an entire year, where I could communicate and connect with him more personally than just through email, and I knew this was exactly what I needed. I signed up to work with Micah and signed up my wife, Miriam, to work with Diana for the year. I knew that the two of us working together to improve would be even better than if I took this journey alone.

By the end of May 2024, just a few short months after the conference, Miriam and I were attending the SoulFIT Retreat in Mexico. I had lost around sixty pounds since the conference, but more importantly, I was in the process of reclaiming my life. The retreat wasn't just about fitness; it was about healing. I wanted this, but I always thought it could make me look weak. But what I saw from Micah and the community of people at SoulFIT was that vulnerability takes tremendous courage, and healing was an incredibly hard journey that required incredible strength.

I saw men opening up about all different types of pain. Micah's openness about his trauma freed us up to share about the things we each had to deal with. Even though the experiences weren't exactly the same as Micah's, the shame, the guilt, and the desperate desire to numb the pain with coping tools that ended up causing harm was a common theme.

I realized that Micah and this SoulFIT community genuinely wanted the best for me. After the retreat in Mexico, I connected with a life coach (who was one of the group mentors), and for the first time in years, I opened up. I got vulnerable.

That was a turning point.

Micah helped me see that it's okay for men to struggle and to speak about it. With his guidance, and the support of my life coach, I reconnected with my faith. I rebuilt my relationship with my wife and kids. I learned to shut off from work and be present. I began to cultivate a healthy relationship with food, with fitness, and with myself.

I went from being a 300-pound, overworked, addicted man on the verge of losing everything to a 215-pound, mentally strong, emotionally grounded husband, father, and leader.

I used to think success was measured by revenue, profit, or business valuation. But true success, I've learned, is measured by the *quality of your relationship with God, family and friends, the time you invest in your loved ones, and the impact you make in the lives of others.*

Today, I live with peace, not because everything is perfect but because I finally know what truly matters.

27

FINISH WHAT YOU STARTED

It was 5 a.m., and like clockwork, the monkeys started whooping and hollering, announcing that it was time to get up and start the day.

I smiled as soon as I heard them, lifted my head off the pillow, and looked out the window across beautiful Lake Arenal in Costa Rica. The signs of dawn were beginning, and soon the morning would be filled with the sounds of hundreds of birds. The toucans are my favorite, and here in this spot in the mountains of Costa Rica, my place of preference to celebrate my birthday, we see them nearly every day.

This year, 2024, my birthday felt different. I had a deeper sense of purpose now than I had ever experienced. Since the weight of sharing my story had been lifted, I felt like I was ready to run. Diana and I had taken some time to recover, rest, and relax after the conference. She needed the break, especially after this event. Diana had sunk into a sadness unlike her; she knew it wasn't normal, and she was fighting back, but ultimately, the Lord had just told her to rest. So it had been a few weeks of rest, refreshment, and recovery, and that time also coincided with this birthday trip to Costa Rica, a spot where time feels like it just slows down.

On one of the last days of our trip, we went to a favorite spot to close out our time with massages. Once finished, the windows of the massage room open up to display a glorious view of the Arenal volcano. The big reveal never gets old!

I tend to fall asleep during massages, but Diana is the opposite, and this time was no different. Her mind starts whirling as she lies there; the relaxation boosts her creative mind.

We emerged from the spa, and she looked at me and said, "God spoke to me in there." As you well know by now, when Diana says this, I listen.

"He said, *Finish what you started*," she told me. "He meant, it's time to finish your book."

I smiled for two reasons. One, my wife was back in action. I could tell that her batteries, which the conference had depleted, were now recharged, and she was ready to go. Two, I smiled because I had been feeling it too. I knew it was time to get my story crafted so I could reach other men and women out there who needed my help.

———

Diana began working on my story in 2015, long before I embarked on my healing journey. She even drafted a book proposal and took it to a conference for female authors and speakers called She Speaks, where she had the chance to pitch it to publishers. One woman, representing a major publisher, had shown great interest, and I even had the chance to go in and meet her in person. Now I didn't actually attend the conference; I hung out at the hotel, found gyms to work out at, and chicken to eat, while she went to classes and listened to various speakers. But when she had her publisher meeting, Diana wanted me to hang out in the hallway, just in case there was interest and someone wanted to meet me. Her hunch was right.

It was encouraging. And even though it ended up being a no, it was exciting to know that it had sparked interest. The publisher emphatically told us to continue on the journey and that it was a story that needed to be told. The timing for the story was off anyway, so the rejection was actually a great relief. My healing journey had barely begun, and there was so much more to come, but this whole experience was a little God wink assuring us that it would happen when the time was right.

So when Diana heard *"Finish what you started,"* she was completely clear about what that meant. It was time to dig in and start writing and crafting this story.

When we returned from Costa Rica, Diana started working on the book. Every day, she would sit and write and then come and read it to me, ensuring that my thoughts, words, and feelings were being captured correctly.

We were in a fantastic rhythm. This project was going to get done. God had big plans for me, and as soon as we published the book, I could step in and get started on this new work. I couldn't wait.

This story was finished.

Or so I thought.

What I didn't see coming was one more gigantic, terrifying step the Lord needed me to take.

There were more chapters to be written.

My dad, a rockstar in real life, in full Alice Cooper gear with his band, Strictly Alice.

Cover of the local paper at age five.

California trip age ten, seeing the ocean for the first time.

My Big Brother, Bill, from Big Brothers Big Sisters who guided me.

Homecoming at fifteen; it came with a hidden cost.

Eighteen years old and 138 pounds, ready for change.

My fitness journey began when I got to college.

My good friend David who inspired me to be a fitness model.

My first fitness cover after eight years of hard work.

The comeback cover after my car accident.

Filming a pilot for The Janice Dickinson Modeling Agency.

The first day I met Diana.

Launching Hitch Fit Online Training and Hitch Fit Gym together.

Our wedding day was filled with joy.

Turning my heart back to the Lord through Diana's love.

The Muscle & Fitness *feature that connected us.*

Landing my dream cover on Ironman, *the magazine that once inspired me.*

My first national TV appearance on CTN.

Using national TV to share hope and inspire others.

My friend Bill and his family saved my life in high school.

Nolan is a lifelong friend who always stood by my side.

My forge of brothers Adam, Matt, and Mitch.

Rob after losing 115 pounds and becoming a new man.

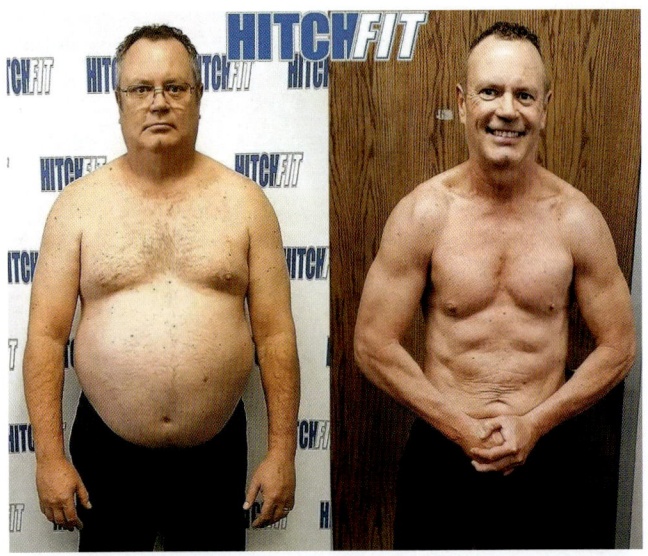

Rob's journey inspired thousands more.

Ben's transformation brought strength and freedom from anxiety.

Ben became a good friend.

Ricky lost eighty-five pounds.

Ricky's whole life was changed.

We dressed as superheroes in Vegas to support Atlas Free.

The first day I began writing about my healing journey.

My wife covering me in prayer before I spoke.

On stage releasing my testimony.

My wife in prayer covering me while I spoke.

Stepping off stage being embraced by Jason and my father-in-law, Frank.

After speaking, all attendees laid hands on me as Markus prayed over me.

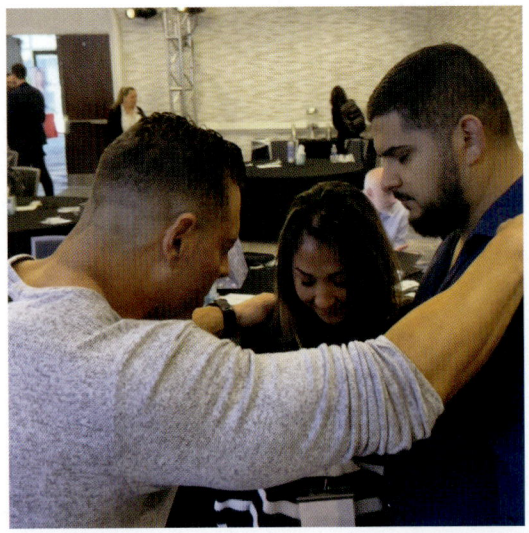

Moments later I prayed for Ricky and Miriam.

Diana started writing my book, The Breaker.

Returning to the house where I had been abused and finding it gone.

God had erased that place from the earth.

Leading another life-changing SoulFIT retreat.

Our retreat group prayed over me before I appeared in court.

Prayer circles around the courthouse before I faced my Goliath.

Over fifteen hundred people were praying for me that day.

Moments before stepping into the courtroom.

The next day, hiking a breathtaking trail and thanking the Lord.

True freedom at last.

Traveling the world with Diana and praising God from mountaintops.

A climb that terrified me and changed my view of fear.

Free from the weight I had carried for decades.

New goals and new challenges.

New places and new memories.

Seeing God's beauty.

Down on one knee again ten years after getting married with the ring I had always wanted to give Diana.

Creating life-changing experiences for others.

Our kids in Haiti.

In Mexico, a boy asked me how to build big muscles. Chicken and dumbbells!

I met this young man in the airport, and he showed me his strength.

Flex and smile young one.

One of the best days of my life was meeting our kids in Haiti.

This boy had just lost his father.

My mission is to lift others higher.

The power of prayer.

Baptized together in the ocean.

Meeting Ed Mylett, one of my favorite speakers.

Launching A Few Things *podcast with Diana.*

Tim Tebow, a warrior for the Lord.

First draft of The Breaker *completed.*

Light always pierces the darkness from pain to purpose.

The moment I told Bill what happened to me and how his family had saved my life.

28

THE CALL

The phone rang as Diana and I settled in for dinner and a movie in April, 2024.

I didn't recognize the number, but the words "Washington State" were displayed across the face of my phone. For some reason, just seeing them made my heart skip a beat.

I didn't answer. Maybe it was a spam call, I thought to myself.

An alert popped up on my phone letting me know I had a new voicemail, I immediately clicked to listen.

A lump rose in my throat, and I looked wide-eyed at Diana.

"It's a lawyer from Washington," I told her. Her jaw dropped.

"What? You're kidding?"

I dialed the number.

My call was answered quickly.

"Hi, this is Micah LaCerte. I just got your message and am calling you back."

The man on the line said he was trying to contact my mother.

"Did she do something?" I asked.

"Oh, no," he responded. "We're trying to find her to see if she would be a witness in a case."

The investigator asked if I would call the prosecuting attorney in charge of the case.

"Of course," I answered.

He shared the attorney's information with me, and we ended the call.

"What the heck is going on?" Diana asked. We both just looked at each other. My stomach was in knots as my mind tried to navigate what this call was going to be about. But in my heart, I already knew.

I called the prosecuting attorney and connected with him instantly. I asked if he could just fill me in on what was going on. His answers revealed that my instincts were accurate.

Kenny had been released from jail after serving thirteen years for what he did to me and the six other boys who came forward all those years ago. After being out of jail for several years, he was back in custody for suspicious behavior. Although he couldn't reveal many details, the prosecuting attorney was seeking character witnesses who could testify at his trial, which would be held in just a couple of months.

Diana stood next to me, listening to every word. We were both in a bit of shock. What is happening? Here we are, in the midst of writing this story, thinking that this saga is over, and ready to get out there and help others. And now this?

The attorney asked if he could call me back in a few minutes to get his partner on the phone to be a part of the conversation.

As we waited for him to call back, Diana and I just sat in the living room together, not quite knowing what to think or say.

Lord, what is it you need me to do? I'll be obedient to whatever it is. It was slowly dawning on me that this could mean facing Kenny again.

I know the Lord won't hand me anything more than I can handle. The timing of this was unquestionably divine. Just a few months earlier, I stood on a stage and shared my story in a large public venue for the first time. The chains of silence, fear, shame, and guilt had all been broken. Though this was a curveball, I had calm and peace, knowing that whatever this step looked like, I would take it, and trust that it would lead to even more impact than I could imagine.

As we got back on the phone, this time with two detectives, Diana and I listened as they shared details with us from the testimony my mother and I had both given back when I was 19 years old for Kenny's first conviction. They were filling us in on dates that I hadn't been certain of and verifying ages and details that I would never have been sure of without their help.

The attorney apologized for digging up old wounds. But I told him, "You have no idea. You're giving me answers and clarity, and I'm literally in the process of writing my book so I can help others, especially men who have gone through trauma." I let him know that God had been a big part of my healing path and I was prepared to use my testimony to help others break free too.

At the mention of faith, knowing we were on the same page, the attorney began sharing from the book of Job and then Romans. *Oh my goodness*, I thought, *he is a believer*. Diana and I looked at each other, shook our heads in amazement, and smiled. Wow, God, wow.

As he shared from the records of the former trial, my testimony and my mother's, it felt like he was reading out of my book.

Then came the moment that took my breath away.

"Micah, in your mother's testimony, she stated that you told her about the abuse when you were ten, but then when you were fifteen, you said you were stronger now, so you would be fine to go back to Kenny's house. So she sent you back in."

I froze. I looked at Diana, and we covered our mouths to muffle the sobs. Tears welled up in our eyes as we looked at each other in disbelief.

She knew. My mother knew. She even gave testimony that she knew and then sent me back.

Until that moment, I just hadn't been sure. I thought I remembered telling her after the first incident, but then I thought I must be mistaken because surely if she had known, she wouldn't have sent me to Kenny again. No mother would do that. No parent in their right mind would let their child go back, even if they said they were bigger and stronger and would be fine.

The words hurt. When the attorney stopped speaking, I struggled to let him know the insight he had just given me. I had been wondering for so long, and now I knew, without a doubt. He apologized for stirring something else up, but I thanked him. Though I had hoped and prayed for years that this wasn't true, at least I no longer had to wonder.

We spoke with the two detectives for over an hour. I shared what I knew, and the path God had set me on, and they listened. They were blown away.

Multiple times, they shared that this was so unusual, not only to find a victim who was willing to speak up and speak out but also one who had done enough healing to be at a point of wanting to help others who had gone through abuse as well. Especially being a man.

There would be a trial, and they needed me to come and testify and share my story and experience. Would I do it?

"Yes, of course, anything I need to do to help, I'm in."

I contrasted this response with what I had felt all those years before, knowing now that it was August 1998 when the first detective had come to me seeking my testimony. The fear of sharing at that time stemmed from not wanting to be exposed and for people to discover what had happened. Now, here I was, all these years later, ready to share, without hesitation. I can only attribute that to the work of God in me.

When the conversation finally ended, Diana and I looked at each other in disbelief as we let this new reality settle in.

My mother knew.

This was going to be a tough one to process. I felt anger and hurt rising. Diana looked at me sympathetically. She could see how deeply this hurt, and she gently reminded me, "Your mother wasn't mentally well."

"God, I'm going to need your help with this," I whispered in prayer. I knew I would need to get to a place of forgiveness for her, which would take some time, but I also knew I was equipped to get there. As I had done with Kenny, I would choose to forgive her and not let any root of bitterness take hold of my heart.

The second thing that needed to sink in was that I would have to go to a trial and face Kenny again. From what they told me, he would be in the room as I shared what he had put me through.

I started praying, "Lord, I need you. Lord, give me courage. Lord, give me the strength."

And I knew that He would.

The Micah from seven years ago couldn't have done this. I wasn't strong enough then. I hadn't gone through the necessary battles to prepare for this level. I would have frozen in fear at this new challenge—the fear of exposure, the fear of shame, the fear of people finding out and knowing about this deep, dark secret. But no, God waited until I was ready. He waited until the chains of fear and shame had been shattered. He waited until I had been released enough that I could step in with no hesitation and say *yes* to the next trial that was in store.

And this time, it was *literally* a trial.

29

HATE OR HEALING

"Hello Mr. LaCerte, I'm the defense attorney for Kenny."

The first step leading into the trial was a phone deposition. The attorney defending Kenny would have a chance to question me, review my story, and get a sense of where I was mentally and emotionally, determining what questions they would want to ask when I took the stand.

Leading into this moment, I had done even more soul-searching. Months ago, on a walk with Diana, we had discussed forgiveness, and I truly felt that I had reached that point with Kenny. But now it was time to put that forgiveness to the test. Had I *really* forgiven him? Is that what would come out during this call? Or would I find hints of the hatred that had once consumed me still lingering?

As I prepared for this deposition, I asked the Lord to search my heart. When I recall moments in my abuse, I am still disgusted. I don't believe that will ever go away. But the disgust no longer has shame attached to it. With Kenny, I had forgiven, but that was easy to say when it wasn't likely that I would have to see him again. Now, to come face-to-face with him in court—what would that feel like?

Before the call, I knew I needed to make sure my heart posture was right. I realized that I had a huge opportunity to be a part of this trial. But the opportunity wasn't to strike out in revenge against Kenny and what he had done to me.

That would, of course, be a normal and natural response. The chance to "get him" for the pain he had caused, the innocence he had stolen. But I realized that wasn't why God was giving me this stand. God says that vengeance is up to Him. It's not my job. It's not something I have to worry about.

What He needed of me was to show up, with a heart surrendered under His love, and to show what it looks like to forgive instead of harboring anger, to choose healing over hatred.

Any man could take the stand full of anger, hatred, and vengeance, and all of those feelings would be justified in the opinion of the world or anyone watching.

But even more powerful would be a man showing up with a spirit of forgiveness and grace. That wouldn't mean that whatever new abuses Kenny had chosen to inflict wouldn't have consequences. Rather, it would be a sign of release and freedom for those who had gone through abuse.

The strongest, most powerful thing I could do was forgive and pray that Kenny would come to a place of true repentance for his actions. I prayed that he would be so convicted that he would turn from his wickedness and turn to God for forgiveness.

Before the deposition call, Diana and I prayed and worshipped together. I just prayed for the peace I would need for that conversation and for the right words to flow.

And they did.

I weaved through detail after detail of my abuse and relationship with Kenny. The attorney was respectful, apologizing for asking me questions that he knew were painful and uncomfortable.

"How do you regard Kenny at this point of your life?" the defense attorney questioned.

"I've come to a place of forgiveness through Jesus, through healing. I pray for him. I had to work through the vengeance and anger I held for many years. I couldn't hate and heal at the same time. So I chose to heal. And through that was forgiving Kenny for what he did to me."

As the words came out, I knew it was really true. I felt it in my heart. I had released Kenny.

I was ready to take the stand.

30
PREPARING FOR BATTLE

"The trial date's been set," the prosecuting attorney let me know.

It was sooner than I thought. Diana and I were preparing to host our SoulFIT Retreat in Mexico. The trial date would mean we would fly home from Mexico, spend two days in Kansas City, and then head to Washington.

Truthfully, I was grateful that I wouldn't have to wait. I had dreams of seeing Kenny again and what that moment would be like, and though I was ready for it, I just wanted to get it over with.

I didn't know how the flow of the trial would go, but I hoped I would get the chance to look him in the eye and tell him that even though he had done evil to me, I had forgiven him and that I hoped that he would come to repentance and turn from his wicked ways.

Our Mexico retreat was incredible. We had nearly fifty people, and we truly couldn't have asked for things to go better. With the foundation of faith and fitness that we infuse into every retreat experience, it was a beautiful time of restoration, connection, and healing for everyone who joined us.

I shared my story with the group and the next step I would be taking in just a few short days. The outpouring of support, love, and prayers from our group mentors and every attendee was overwhelming.

One of the most amazing things was that Diana and I, despite running the event and doing all the "things" to make sure it flowed well, weren't exhausted and depleted. In fact, by the end of the time, we felt refreshed ourselves. That was truly a gift from God. He knew that we both would need strength and energy for the trip to Washington.

After checking into the hotel in Seattle, we headed to a bodybuilder gym nearby to hit the weights and release the feelings of stress that were popping up. The trial would be the next day, so Diana and I had plenty of time to train and to relax, and we planned to walk over to the courthouse that afternoon so that we could do seven prayer circles around the building. (In the book of Joshua in the Bible, there is a battle at the wall of Jericho.[9] God's instruction to win the battle was to march around the city for six days, and then, on the seventh day, the soldiers marched seven times, and the walls fell.) Walking around the building seven times as we prayed was our way of claiming victory over this battle.

On the way to the courthouse, I got an amazing surprise. Diana had been scheming with our dear friend, an amazing speaker and coach, and one of my spiritual mentors, Brent Stromme. He had flown up to Washington to surprise and be with me during the trial. He was nonchalantly standing in front of one of the hotels on our trek toward the courthouse. I walked right by him at first, but when I heard a familiar voice say "Hey!" I turned and lit up like a Christmas tree.

Diana, of course, captured the whole thing on video and giggled as Brent and I embraced. Then, he joined us for our prayer walk.

Two other friends, Rob and Kimberly Skinner, were flying in that evening as well to be with Diana and me and give us their love and support. I was overwhelmed that these amazing humans would take their time to be there for me.

31
PROMOTION DAY

The day of the trial dawned.

I woke up at my usual 3 a.m. and worked out at the hotel gym.

Diana sat in the room, reflecting and praying, and when I got back, she shared with me what the Lord had spoken to her heart.

"Listen to this," she said as she started reading.

"Micah shall rise up as a man of valor, he shall be a mentor to many young men. He is like David, a man after my own heart. Like you, he shall breathe life back into those that were broken and defeated. He will teach them how to war in prayer. They shall be attracted to his outside stature, but I shall cause their eyes to open and they shall see him as who he is meant to be in the Spirit. For I have called him to be a general in my Army, and your household will come to great acclaim."

I'd heard these words before. Years ago, a friend wrote Diana a prophetic letter. She keeps that letter in her journal and reads it regularly as new things unfold in her life. These words about me were a part of that letter.

She continued, "We've always known this was true, that there was something more. To be a general in the army, you must serve for twenty to thirty years. You must go through massive battles and be disciplined and persistent for a long time. You must have the favor of man and God to get there too. Jesus and David both had that favor. It's essential for promotion.

"I believe today's your promotion day, stepping into that general's role after battles most would flee. It's a massive responsibility to step into that role, but it takes a lot to even just be able to come to the point of being promoted to that level."

She paused for a moment and sat thoughtfully. I stayed silent and listened as she continued, taking in every word.

"Today is a gift. Having forgiveness in your heart is so powerful because it is only through God's grace and mercy that we can come to a point of forgiveness for horrible things that have been done. But God has forgiven us of everything. To truly show His light, we must walk in forgiveness so bitter roots don't take hold in our hearts. Bitterness digs deep if unchecked, choking out life, light, peace, joy, healthy minds, and healthy relationships.

"Forgiveness is one step, and I realized another step just now. We are coming at this from a spirit and heart of forgiveness, but there's another level. There's forgiveness, and then there's adding to that gratitude. Gratitude for the outcome of the pain that you've gone through. As horrible as your abuse was, Micah, without those dark depths and leaning on God, you wouldn't be this man today. And that is something for which we can be incredibly grateful.

"I was thinking of David and Goliath. People think it's an underdog story. But David didn't think he was an underdog. He wasn't timidly thinking, *Maybe I'll win*, he was like, 'I'm going to win this; what are you all worried about?' He didn't see this giant as scary. He had no fear because he knew the Lord was on his side. He also knew the skill set he had honed after years of being a shepherd. He had defeated bears and lions with his bare hands. He was so skilled with the sling, which looked small, but it was a deadly weapon. He didn't go into that battle with wavering confidence because he *knew* he wasn't the underdog.

"And when he killed that giant, what happened then? All these armies of men had been cowering, fearful, and afraid to fight the giant who was threatening their lives and holding them in bondage to fear. But now, instead of running, they surged forward into the battle. David's victory gave them confidence to fight too.

"I feel like that's where we are, Micah. It's your time to be like David. You're no underdog. You have the Lord on your side. He masterfully turned something the enemy did to you to try to destroy you and turned it into a means of building incredible strength. It's like David when that lion came to destroy him, growling, clawing, and maybe even sinking its teeth into him. He fought back, and he killed it, and he was stronger for having to fight that battle.

"God has equipped you for years with the skill set that you need for this war, this position as general. And when you defeat this enemy and show these other men and women that it can be done, that this giant can be crushed, they will surge forward in battle and not be afraid to fight."

All I could say in response to Diana's beautiful words was "Amen." God had prepared us for this battle, and because of His love and grace and power, the victory was already won.

32

LIGHT ON THE STAND

"Right this way, Mr. LaCerte."

Diana, our tribe of friends, and I entered the courthouse and followed the sweet lady from our prosecuting attorney's team as she led us through security and navigated us through the halls of the grand building.

Everything felt a bit surreal, but I had a sense of peace. Not only did I have a crew of loved ones by my side but I had shared on social media that I was going through something challenging. Even without going into detail, over fifteen hundred people reached out to me, letting me know they were praying for me even though they didn't know the specifics. I felt the power of those prayers.

Diana and I held hands tightly as we took the elevator up and then headed down the polished white marble floors to the waiting room that was prepared for us.

We met the prosecuting attorney and the rest of the team I'd been communicating with over the past few months. Everyone was warm and welcoming and consistently expressed gratitude for my willingness to be there.

About ten minutes before we were summoned to the courtroom, one of the team members came in and informed me that Kenny had opted not to be in the room for my testimony. It came as a bit of a shock, as I didn't realize that was an option. He would be watching and listening on Zoom but didn't want to have to face me in that room.

I was prepared to face him and had believed I was going to have to, so in my heart, I had a bit of disappointment. But I was at such a place of surrender to the Lord that I trusted that whatever the situation was, it was part of His plan. Maybe all He had needed from me was to know I would say yes, that I would look Kenny in the eye, and when I did that, He made it so I didn't have to. Knowing that he would hear my words was enough.

We all entered the courtroom. Diana and my friends took a seat in the back and I made my way up to the witness stand. I had never been in a courtroom with a jury before, and I was surprised at how small everything seemed. The jury box was to my immediate left, and it was *very* close—so close that one of the jurors was just a couple of feet from me, and for a moment, I felt a surge of discomfort knowing I was about to share some of the darkest moments of my life with a stranger staring at me. But I took a deep breath and let that go. I was here because it's where God needed me to be, and I was going to do this.

The jury looked at me, then at Diana, and back at me. It felt like they were trying to make sense of us. I had a feeling they hadn't seen too many bodybuilders in that setting.

The judge was kind, and once we were all settled, the process began.

For an hour, with the gently guided questions from my attorney, I weaved through the details of my story for the judge and jury, knowing that Kenny heard every word. Once I started speaking, the words just flowed. I wasn't nervous, I wasn't afraid. I felt a sense of peace come over me. Since the past no longer held me in bondage, I was able to share openly and with vulnerability without getting stuck in pain.

The trial concluded with barely a question from the defense attorney.

"No further questions, your honor."

It was over.

As we left the courthouse, it felt like another enormous weight had been lifted.

I don't know why the Lord needed me to take that step, and I will never know the full impact of the story I shared that day on this side of heaven. However, I know the Lord asked me to do it, and I said yes.

I also know I'm supposed to help people in different ways, and on deeper levels than I ever have before. I know this ministry will look different, and even though I have ideas of what I think will happen, I've got a sneaking suspicion that God's got something much more in store than I can even begin to imagine.

A big chunk of my life was spent in darkness. But it's now my time to be a light. I had the chance to take a *literal* "stand" and shine a light on the darkness of sexual abuse.

Matthew 5:14–16 says, "You are the light of the world. A town built on a hill cannot be hidden. Neither do people light a lamp and put it under a bowl. Instead they put it on its stand, and it gives light to everyone in the house. In the same way, let your light shine before others, that they may see your good deeds and glorify your Father in heaven."[10]

What happens when you enter a dark room and flick on the light? The darkness flees. Darkness doesn't have a chance against light. It's not even a competition. The light wins every time.

33
MY SUPERPOWER

From the time I was a young boy until now, I've always wanted to be a superhero.

One of my favorite video games is *The Legend of Zelda*, in which you fight evil and save the princess with the whole world on the line.

For those unfamiliar with *Zelda*, the main character is Link. He starts off weak. He has no armor, skills, or weapons. Throughout the game, he battles enemies and goes through trials and challenges. If he fights a battle and loses, he has to fight again. He can't progress until that battle is won. But each time he faces the same enemy, he understands them better and is more equipped to defeat them.

As Link progresses through the game, he becomes stronger, gaining new abilities and access to weapons. He starts with a small wooden sword. Each victory throughout the game, each enemy defeated, upgrades his gear until he eventually acquires the coveted Master Sword, one of the weapons that can defeat the final enemy boss and save the world.

Link doesn't have the skills or strength at the beginning of the game to handle the Master Sword. It would be impossible for him to be the hero of the story if he skipped the multitude of battles and unforeseen challenges that lay ahead. He *has* to go through them.

I started out like Link: small, breakable, no armor. I had to fight every battle, storm, and setback to build the strength I need for today.

I've had people come up to me and kindly say, "I'm so sorry this happened to you."

My response now is, "Thank you for that, but I'm not sorry it happened any longer."

I appreciate the sentiment, and I know they are telling me this because they care about me. And I know that response may sound absurd. It's just that I see things so differently now; I view my abuse through an entirely different lens. I get it: Most survivors would think I'm nuts not to be sorry it happened, to even feel gratitude for it now. Let me explain.

I went through something horrific, something that no child or adult should ever have to endure. I don't want anyone to go through what I did, and my heart breaks for those who have faced similar situations at any level. I'm not grateful that I was abused, but I'm so grateful for the healing journey that I had to go through, the massive strength I gained because of it, and the person I have become. From that hell of pain and struggle, I forged a superpower. I can understand what other victims have gone through and show them a pathway of hope and victory.

That is what I'm grateful for—the opportunity to be a part of the solution to a crippling problem and the ability to be a powerful voice in a space where silence has often reigned.

I get to be a hero.

I'm here to save lives, maybe even change the world.

34

THE BREAKER

One in six.

Walking down a crowded street or into a room full of people, my perspective has changed through my healing journey. I know that statistically, one out of every six men in that room and one out of every four women have experienced something similar to what I have.

I'd bet those numbers are higher—men, especially, tend to bury it deeper, staying silent their whole lives.

I've seen how trauma ripples through every aspect of life. I know firsthand how those unhealed wounds show up in the forms of anger, addiction, overachieving, broken relationships, and so many other symptoms.

I know there are millions of people suffering from the chains of bondage from past abuse and living in the wake of the effects of trauma. It's time we started breaking those chains.

One morning in January 2025, Diana was doing her devotions. She skimmed a passage and nothing clicked, but then the same verse popped up in her devotion time the next day. This time, it halted her in her tracks. Her eyes widened as she read the words, absorbing each one. Her heart started to race a little faster, realizing that the Lord had just given her yet another piece of this book.

> The breaker [the Messiah, who opens the way] shall go up before them [liberating them]. They will break out, pass through the gate and go out; so their King goes on before them, the Lord at their head. (Micah 2:13)[11]

The Breaker. That's what this verse refers to Jesus as: "the Breaker" who goes first and breaks through. He smashes the walls of bondage, unshackles the chains, and paves the way so we can walk in freedom behind Him.

Wow. She racked her brain, trying to think of any time she had heard of Jesus called "the Breaker" in the past. She started looking it up and discovered that this short verse in Micah was the only place in the Bible where Jesus the Messiah was referred to as the Breaker.

As she was soaking this in, a tiny, super obvious detail that had eluded her until that moment came to light. "Oh my goodness, it's in the book of *Micah*," she said aloud and then laughed at the oversight.

Yes, it took her *that* long to catch that the verse was in Micah! I will give her a little grace; she hadn't had any coffee yet!

I was at the gym when these revelations were flooding in for my wife. My phone started blowing up with text messages as she couldn't wait to share what she had discovered.

I read her texts and it hit me too. Jesus is the Breaker. It was in the book of Micah. Holy smokes, this was amazing.

As soon as I finished with clients, I pulled up Micah on my phone and started reading chapter 2. My jaw dropped yet again when I read the first verse.

"Woe (judgment is coming) to those who devise wickedness and plot evil on their beds! When morning comes, they practice evil because it is in the power of their hands."[12]

I gulped hard. This verse nails its, straight at predators like Kenny, plotting evil in the dark.

But then, in verse 13, Hope enters the story in the form of Jesus, the Breaker.

I was a captive for a long time, but those chains are broken by the grace of Jesus, the Breaker, who went before me and created the path for me. I am a free man.

Those chains cut deep, and my scars remain, but they are healed. Those will never disappear, and I have no shame about them, and I no longer try to hide them. Do you have an open wound, a scab, or a scar too? You don't have to be ashamed either.

I'm on a mission. I call it The Breaker Mission, which is, in other words, the Jesus Mission. When I read Isaiah 61:1, my mission snapped into focus.

> The Spirit of the Lord is on me, because I am marked by Him to give good news to the poor (in spirit); He has sent me to make the broken-hearted well, to say that the prisoners will be made free, and that those in chains will see the light again.[13]

These words were for me (and maybe they are for you too). I knew this was what Jesus had done for me, and it was what I was called to do for others.

Let me tell you something else about this verse, because this is how incredible God is. The day after Diana and I set up the legal formation paperwork for The Breaker Mission, she was led to Isaiah 61 for her devotion time and realized an even deeper message for us from this verse.

In the textual notes in her Bible, next to Isaiah 61:1, it says, "Jesus Began Here." His mission began with this exact message.[14] If that's where He started, that's where we start too.

He broke through so that I could break through and lead the charge for others. Perhaps you're one of them.

I know that some of you reading this have gone through some level of abuse or a traumatic experience like I have. You might've been on your healing journey for a while or are just starting one. Maybe you've been consumed by fear, shame, and guilt and haven't been able to share yet. Or maybe you would like to share but haven't found a safe space or person to confide in to take that first step.

Regardless of where you are, the most important thing I can tell you is that there is Hope. I use a capital *H* for a reason. I'm not talking about the type of hope that is wishful thinking, along the lines of "I hope someday I heal." I'm talking about Hope as an expectation. It's something that is certain and anticipated. It's going to happen.

Healing is available, and there is a God who loves you immensely, is the Source of Hope, and wants to be a part of your healing. There's healing for your brokenness and your wounds; no matter how messy you think your situation is, it's not too much for Him. Your chains can be broken.

For those of you who have undergone healing, you may now be ready to harness your superpower by helping others and finding purpose in the painful experiences you've gone through. If you are doing that, I'd love to hear from you.

For those who are in the process of healing, keep at it. The pace of your journey doesn't matter; sticking with it does.

For those who haven't shared yet, maybe it's time to take that first step with a safe person or group.

I can tell you firsthand that it's not an easy journey, but it is worth every step.

I'm grateful you've come this far with me. Thank you for hearing my story and holding it with me. You're part of this wild, healing tapestry that God has woven through my life.

As I bring this story to a close, I invite you to join me for one final piece of my healing path. There was one last place I needed to visit. I was a bit anxious about what I would say and how I would feel. But I knew it was time to take the inward journey. I was ready to go back and meet with the younger me.

35
THE TRAIN

I saw him sitting alone on the train—his face pressed to the window, his eyes watching the world rushing by.

I knew his racing thoughts and the fear clawing at him.

He was bigger and stronger now. He thought surely the horror of sexual abuse wouldn't happen to him again.

I knew he was wrong.

A lump caught in my throat as I watched him.

I knew what he was about to go through. I knew the years of shame, anger, hurt, and healing that lay ahead. I knew his pain would come close to taking his life, but I also knew that, by God's grace, it wouldn't.

I walked slowly down the aisle toward him, and when I reached his seat, I said, "Can I sit next to you?"

He turned from the window and looked up at me. His jaw dropped. He smiled and nodded while staring at my biceps.

I laughed because I knew he had never seen anyone that looked like me in person. He dreamed of looking like Jean-Claude Van Damme someday, and I was the closest to that he'd ever seen.

I took the seat next to him and smiled as he sat tall and tried to puff himself up.

"How did you get so strong?" he asked.

I paused for a moment, thinking of how loaded that question was. He was just thinking of my biceps. I was thinking of all the strength built in every way in the thirty-plus years since the younger me sat on that train.

He waited for an answer. I locked eyes with him and could see his sincere curiosity, coupled with the fears, doubts, and feelings of weakness, swirling through his mind. I looked at his smile, the one that I knew masked so much pain.

"How did I get so strong?" I thoughtfully repeated his question.

"It took years of grinding and lifting heavy weights. I started small and weak, barely able to hoist a bar. I had to begin with what I could handle, and over time, I kept getting stronger. A weight that felt heavy just a couple of weeks before started to feel lighter, and then I was able to lift more.

"Lifting heavy tears your muscles; that stings at first. But as they heal, they grow tougher. You have to break it down to build it up.

"I learned I didn't have to lift alone. People I trusted helped me lift that weight when I got stuck. Asking for help and allowing others to spot me gave me the strength to push heavier weights and helped me grow stronger than I could have on my own."

He sat silently, taking in every word.

"That's how I've become so strong. Heavy weights, help from others, and healing."

He looked at me and nodded. "I hope I can be as strong as you someday."

I looked up to the front of the train and took a deep breath. There was so much more that I wanted to share with him.

"You know what? You will.

"Life is the same grind, like Zelda, starting weak against monsters too big to beat."

His eyes lit up at the mention of his favorite video game.

"Those monsters are heavy weights, huge, crushing at first glance. You feel helpless and hopeless, thinking it's impossible to have the strength to move them.

"But you're not alone. God is always there. He never leaves you and never stops loving you, no matter how hard life gets, how heavy the weight feels, or how unbeatable that monster seems. He'll back you up on every lift.

"It feels brutal at first, but you push through and build up a little more muscle for the next tough thing that comes along. When you reach that sticking point, you won't build more strength unless you reach out for help. That's when you ask for it, and you'll see that God has placed people around you who are going to help you lift that weight and get even stronger."

I looked over at him, knowing this was a lot to share, but seeing that he was absorbing every word and taking it to heart. He knew we were talking about so much more than muscles.

His gaze was fixed on me like glue. The pain he had buried inside welled up, brimming his eyes with tears.

He paused for a moment. "Thank you," he said simply.

The train started to slow as we approached the next station.

"This is my stop."

As he grabbed his backpack and got ready to debark, I said, "Hey, before you go, I want you to know this." I pointed to my heart and said, "I see you. I believe in you. You are loved.

"You're stronger than you know. No matter how hard or lonely it feels, you're not alone. You're going to make it through. God has a huge plan and purpose for your life."

He nodded and gave me that smile, then stood and headed toward the exit.

He paused at the door and turned back. His gaze held mine for a moment. Then he stepped off the train and into the crowd.

I looked down at the empty seat next to me, then out the window to catch one last glimpse of him.

He turned back to the train, searching for me. When he saw me in the window, he smiled and waved.

I waved back as a tear of joy welled up in my eye and slid down my cheek.

He wasn't alone.

Right there beside him, with a gentle hand on his shoulder, was Jesus.

The train began to pull away from the station, moving me forward and picking up speed. I leaned back, smiling, as a wave of deep peace washed over me.

PART 2

THE BREAKER'S WAY

My Steps to Healing

36
THE HEALING JOURNEY

"Healing will feel and look different for everyone."

I listened carefully as my friend Candice Raine, CEO of the Arizona Trauma Institute, shared her insights with me.

In the world of fitness, I'm an expert. In the world of trauma recovery, I'm not.

Thankfully, as I've continued to open up and share my story, God has brought resources in the form of books, courses,[15] and incredible people like Candice as well as friends like psychoanalyst Jessica Almond; Licensed Clinical Professional Counselor Bryan Vignery; founder and CEO of Freedom Movement Karrie Scott Garcia; my dear friend, coach, and spiritual mentor Brent Stromme; and others who have helped me process and understand my physiological, psychological, and spiritual journey.

Diana tackled a deeper education in trauma and dug into her own healing so that she would be prepared to facilitate healing journeys for the people we encounter through The Breaker Mission. She is now a Trauma and Resilience Life Coach through the Arizona Trauma Institute and a Biblical Trauma Informed Coach through Freedom Academy.

In the seven years since that Kari Jobe concert, I have undergone significant healing, pushed through immense resistance, and reached a point where I can confidently say I walk in freedom. My past no longer holds me in bondage. Those chains have been broken, and I can share my story and turn all that pain into purpose to help others achieve freedom.

In this second section of the book, I want to share more deeply what my healing process entailed, hoping my steps and process will help others.

So, what exactly are we healing from? What is *trauma*?

Here is a description that resonated with me. According to SAMHSA's Trauma and Justice Strategic Initiative, "trauma results from an event, series of events, or set of circumstances that is experienced by an individual as physically or emotionally harmful or threatening and that has lasting adverse effects on the individual's functioning and physical, social, emotional, or spiritual well-being."[16]

To add my own perspective to that, trauma is a response that happens in our bodies when we've gone through something terrible or when we lose our sense of control. It impacts us to the extent that even after the danger is past or the abuse is no longer happening, our body and brain still respond to the threat as if it's real.

If we don't work toward healing from these past wounds, and we don't learn what is happening in our body and how to manage it so that we can function healthfully, it's possible to live a life entirely controlled by responses to unresolved trauma.

When we experience trauma, especially in childhood, it affects how our nervous system responds and how our brain develops. Our body and brain receive and perceive the world differently than someone who grew up in a stable, safe, and loving environment. Trauma survivors often have a hypervigilant warning system in their brains that causes them to live in heightened states of arousal, which means persistently high levels of stress hormones course through their bodies. Seemingly normal behaviors, when living in these biological conditions, may be impulsive, erratic, or irrational. You may think, *What the heck is wrong with this person? Why are they being a jerk? Is it laziness, or maybe mental illness?* But the truth is that how they are acting is the natural behavior for someone who is experiencing repetitive, chronic high levels of toxic stress from triggers in the world around them.

Living this way can lead to many issues with relationships, health, and the ability to experience a happy and productive life.

Looking back to my high school years, I now understand that the panic attacks and anxiety I was experiencing were normal responses to what was happening in my body. When I was triggered by fear, lack of control of my environment, or a flashback, my brain perceived the threat and gave me a massive dose of stress hormones. I was being triggered multiple times throughout every day, so those stress hormones just kept surging. I was dysregulated, and I didn't know then how to self-regulate to get myself back to a place of calmness in my body. I wasn't mentally ill; I was suffering from the physical and mental symptoms that come as a result of unresolved trauma.

My anger outbursts when I was at home with my mother, the ones that caused her to send me back into the home of a pedophile, weren't because I was a bad kid; they happened because I was a triggered kid. The abuse, the lack of a safe environment at home, and the lack of key stable relationships that I desperately needed in those developmental years caused warning signals to go off in my brain. They were screaming, "NOT SAFE!" and causing surges of stress hormones. The anger and emotional outbursts were the biologically correct response to what was happening in my body and brain.

I had no one in my life who understood, and this realization would take me decades to learn. But when I did find people I could trust and started to recognize trauma responses in my body, I was able to utilize tools and systems to regulate myself to lead a productive life with healthy relationships and a healthy body and mind.

Being trapped in trauma is devastating, but it's sadly how so many people are living, and it's destroying not just the individual but often the people around them too. There's an alternative to living in that bondage, and that's what I'm talking about when I refer to healing.

Each of us has a different healing journey, and the pace of our healing will be different too. My friend Tori Mae Hein, a coach and the executive program and marketing director for Freedom Academy, said something that perfectly summed this up: "Be at peace with the pace that God has for your healing."[17]

As I've emerged from this and can now look back and see how my healing evolved, I've identified six steps, in the order I used them in my life, that got me to the point I'm at today.

As a survivor, a thriver, and a coach, I will share these with you in the next few chapters, along with some of the information and research I've learned. I also asked my friends with more knowledge, wisdom, and education in these areas to share their thoughts and feedback.

If you've gone through abuse, regardless of what type, how long it lasted, or how "bad" you think it was, this is what I want you to know. There is no rush when it comes to healing. You can take things slowly, and your steps might not be the same as mine or in the same order. I encourage you to *take* the steps, but don't worry about how fast you take them or how big those steps are. And don't even worry if you take a step forward and then feel like you take a step back. That's okay too.

Testimony is powerful; I've shared mine throughout this book. When you've gone through something unthinkable, knowing someone else has gone through it and made it to the other side can give you hope. Once you know it's possible, it's a matter of figuring out the pathway to get there.

Looking back through my life, I recognize the pathway I took. Your route will likely look different from mine, or if you have a loved one looking to heal, their journey will not be the same either. But I think it's important to share these actionable steps because *healing will require action*. We cannot sit back and expect it to happen if we do nothing.

And it isn't easy. It's going to take hard work; it's going to take pushing against resistance. But guess what happens when we push against resistance? We get stronger. We build muscle. I built muscle in my physical body that has made me strong and resilient, and I've also built muscle in my mind and spirit, enabling me to tackle life with excitement and purpose. That strength has given me victory in this war and equipped me to be a voice out here, helping other men and women find victory for themselves.

These are the six steps of my healing journey:

1. **Say Something (Speak Up)**
2. **Pursue Fitness and a Structured Lifestyle**
3. **Create a Safe Environment**
4. **Return to Faith/Release Shame and Guilt**
5. **Lean into Forgiveness**
6. **Apply: From Mess to Ministry**

Each of these steps was critical to my recovery process, leading me to the freedom that I walk in today. I believe they can help you too.

I know you will also benefit from the expertise shared by my friends who generously reviewed these steps and gave their professional insight from their varying backgrounds, including professional counselors, trauma experts, psychoanalysts, a therapist, and a pastor.

37
STEP ONE: SAY SOMETHING

As detailed in part 1, when I was fifteen, shame, guilt, embarrassment, and confusion about my abuse consumed me. I didn't want anyone to know what had happened to me. I was terrified of being judged, mocked, and rejected if people discovered the truth. As a young boy, speaking up was the last thing I wanted to do. So I tried to stuff this pain deep inside and throw away the key.

Thankfully, I didn't do that, at least not entirely.

I told my mother about the abuse, and even though she grossly mishandled that information, she didn't call me a liar. She believed that what I said had indeed happened.

Things could have turned out differently if she hadn't believed me. The loss of courage to repeat it, for fear of being told I wasn't telling the truth, may have held me captive and caused massive delays in my future healing journey.

Between the ages of eleven and nineteen, I can count on one hand the number of people that I shared my abuse with. However,

I now realize that the fact that I told *anyone* is extremely rare for a young child.

Numbers from the US Department of Justice suggest that as much as 86 percent of child sexual abuse *never* gets reported.[18] The statistics on how many children are being abused are skewed because of this. The reasons for the lack of reporting are complex and multifaceted, and then there are the reported incidents in which the child was doubted or not believed.

According to the American Psychological Association, the rates of early disclosure of sexual abuse by male survivors is very low; only 10–33 percent of those who tell someone do it when they are still children. Those who disclose later in life wait, on average, twenty-one years to tell anyone, and twenty-eight years to have any in-depth discussion about what they went through.[19]

I was afraid to share, but I'm glad I said something early. I discovered that my fear of sharing was a common theme among the abused.

The National Association of Social Workers' Child Protection Council reported that in 98 percent of the child abuse cases reported to officials, children's statements were found to be true. However, *one in three adults* surveyed by the Australian Childhood Foundation said *they wouldn't believe a child* if that child disclosed sexual abuse.[20]

Sadly, the longer it took to tell someone, the more susceptible these victims were to mental health problems as adults.

Often, perpetrators threaten their victims with harm or harm to those they love if the abuse is revealed. They may threaten that the victim will get in trouble if they tell, or they may use an angle of telling the victim no one will believe them, even if they do say something.

Fear is a powerful deterrent. I feared what people would think. I feared what would happen to Kenny's wife and sons. I feared that I would be thought of as weak. I feared I would be thought of as gay when I wasn't. I feared I would be rejected if people knew what I had gone through.

I didn't want to be seen as a victim. I know now that this is a common fear among men. Statistically, women tend to come forward more frequently and quickly than men do when they have been a victim of sexual abuse; it seems to be "easier" for a woman to acknowledge being a victim than a man.[21] For a man, being a victim implies weakness, a lack of strength and masculinity, and many men choose to suffer in silence, allowing the trauma to seep into other aspects of their lives rather than be named a victim.

Speaking up is surrounded by so much complexity, but as hard as it is, I want to spread the message that it is worth it and that you're not alone.

The CDC estimates that 1 in 4 girls and *1 in 6 boys* will be sexually assaulted by the time they are eighteen years old.[22] And these numbers are likely conservative since, as stated earlier, most cases aren't reported.

As important as it is to tell someone, it is not wise to tell just anyone. It must be a safe person or a safe group or community.

The first people that I shared with were, thankfully, empathetic about what I had gone through and didn't question that I had been abused. My mother, the detective when I was nineteen, the counselor I saw briefly, and an early girlfriend were all safe people for me.

These positive responses were a godsend, but they are not always the case. Say something, yes, but also be discerning about who you share with, especially if you are sharing for the first time. Perhaps it is your spouse, a close friend or relative, a pastor, or a counselor. Find someone who is safe.

Dr. Scott Easton's study of male sexual abuse survivors reported more long-term mental distress if a victim received an unhelpful response when telling someone else about the abuse.[23] Because those

I told accepted and supported me, I didn't experience the shutdown some have endured.

If *you* are the safe person a victim chooses to confide in, please be very intentional and compassionate with your response. Know that how you respond in those critical moments will have a lasting impact, either negatively or positively, on how this individual proceeds in their healing. There are great resources from RAINN (Rape, Abuse and Incest National Network) on how to talk to and respond to a victim of sexual assault who confides in you.[24]

I wouldn't have been capable of healing had I kept my story locked inside. I had to share it. And the work could go forward because those I chose received it with credibility and kindness.

Trauma authority Bessel van der Kolk explains, "When we are unable to process the emotions around the event, they remain stuck in the body and keep us in a perpetual state of helplessness and terror."[25]

To heal, process, and get "unstuck," I had to be heard and get help. But help couldn't come unless I told others I needed it and why.

EXPERT INSIGHTS:

Contribution from Bryan Vignery, Licensed Clinical Professional Counselor

Understanding how sexual abuse affects someone starts with admitting it happened. Sexual abuse can take many forms, and healing looks different for everyone. But one common step in recovering from trauma is shining a light on the hidden corners of our hearts where shame hides. Shame thrives in the dark, but once you bring it into the light, it begins to lose its power, and the stronghold begins to weaken.

When Micah told one person about the abuse he endured, light started to shine on the hidden parts of his heart. That's when his freedom started to come to the surface. Even though there was a lot to work through, I believe that telling that one person thwarted some of the enemy's plans.

Jesus gives us a promise in John 10:10 (NLT): "The thief's purpose is to steal and kill and destroy. My purpose is to give them a rich and satisfying life." The enemy wants to destroy you in many ways, one of which is by keeping the trauma of sexual abuse in the shadows. He does this by making the victim feel defined by shame.

Shame can seem like a protective barrier, but it really just highlights our deep-seated vulnerabilities. It traps us in a cycle where we can't move beyond past pain, keeping us in an emotional prison that can severely impact our mental health. I know that a significant number of people haven't yet acknowledged their own sexual abuse, often because they're struggling with their identity. Unfortunately, this number seems to be as large as those who have already shared their experiences. That's why encouraging those who have been abused to share their stories in a safe setting is so vital. It shines light on shame—and opens the way to healing.

Bryan Vignery, LCPC
https://www.intentionalway.com

38

STEP TWO: MUSCLE PHARMACY

When I was a boy, I imagined myself as a superhero. Amid the abuse, instability in my home, moving incessantly, and a conflict-filled relationship with my mother, it was a way that I coped with the chaos. I imagined that I was saving the day and saving others. My mind escaped to a realm where I was not only safe but strong, in control, and helping others too.

That image stuck. I longed to be stronger. In college, when I discovered the gym and started strength training for the first time, I wanted to build muscle, be strong, and attract girls, but I was also there to be in control. I was there to build armor so that I would never again feel that weakness that I had when Kenny was abusing me.

The thought of the abuse and the anger caged inside of me was released at the gym.

The disciplined regimen I discovered and implemented in my daily rhythm calmed the chaos in my mind.

When I went to the gym to get strong, little did I know that I was learning and implementing a form of self-regulation—a means of bringing my body to a place of calm. Self-regulation is a major key to the healing of trauma. I didn't know it then, but the gym and the powerful way that exercise, and strength training in particular, impacts the brain made it one of the absolute best things I could possibly do for my healing journey. The gym was a means of regulating overwhelming emotions and making them manageable.

What I also didn't realize at that time was that God created a literal pharmacy in our bodies. When I was strength training and contracting my muscles, hormones were being secreted into my body that were positively impacting my mental health and helping me get to a balanced place.

Hitting the weights, as it turns out, had a profound impact on the health of my brain. Exercise, in general, is great, and all of it helps, but studies are showing that weights, in particular, give the biggest bang for your buck when it comes to battling anxiety and depression.[26]

When we exercise, it releases hormones that dramatically impact our levels of "happiness" and ability to function healthfully. These include myokines, dopamine, serotonin, oxytocin, endorphins, and norepinephrine. They all play a role in boosting our mood, reducing stress and anxiety, battling depressive symptoms, and giving us the ability to form healthy relationships with the people around us. The effects don't last forever; as soon as the hormones have done their job, they return to normal. This is why repetition is so important when it comes to exercise. As a daily habit, it is a critical part of the healing process, not just for its strengthening effects on the body but also for its benefits to our brain's healthy functioning.

A 2023 study from the University of South Australia showed physical activity, especially strength training, is *1.5 times more effective* than counseling or medication in treating depression and anxiety.[27]

It's no wonder that I felt so much relief. I craved that sense of calm that came to me when I spent time in the gym training my body. I still do. Nearly thirty years later it remains a critical element of my daily routine.

I wanted more than just the feeling of calm; I also wanted to see results. That meant I couldn't just train and then eat whatever I wanted. I developed disciplined eating structures too. I wanted to eat in order to provide my muscles fuel to grow, and, as it turns out, my healthy nutritional choices were helping with my trauma healing.

Why? Because trauma impacts every system in our body, including our digestive process. And overall nutrition is an important piece of our mental health. More and more studies are finding that changing dietary habits should be a part of the protocol for treating depression.[28]

Eating a healthful diet of whole foods and limiting inflammatory processed foods was healing me from the inside out.

When I was having panic attacks in high school, my stomach was in a constant state of distress. I was afraid to go anywhere that I wouldn't have fast and easy access to a clean bathroom. I ate whatever, including sugar, fast food, and any junk that was given to me. I didn't realize that the unhealthy eating habits were compounding the impact of the trauma in my body and making the anxiety even worse!

I felt the difference in a big way when I later adopted a bodybuilding eating structure. Healthy nutrition was therapy. Here I was, a young guy just trying to build muscle and feel like a normal human being, and I unknowingly incorporated two incredibly powerful healing aids into my lifestyle. Turns out dumbbells and chicken breasts were, in fact, science-backed secrets to my trauma-healing success!

Throughout my journey, I didn't use medication, but if you are healing from trauma, medication may be a part of your process, and there is zero shame in that. Still, from my nonclinical perspective, I would suggest not relying solely on medication. Healthy nutrition habits and regular exercise should be a part of any trauma recovery strategy.

Our bodies are truly remarkable in how they are designed to help us heal. If you're able to implement exercise now, then get started—strength training especially, and that is for both men and women; get a coach if you need help or aren't sure how to train safely. If you need to do some work to get associated with your body first, through counseling or medication, then do that work and start adding the exercise in as soon as you're able.

Working on healthy nutrition habits can be a process too. It's normal for abuse survivors to rely on "comfort" foods that are unhealthy as a way of coping with what's happening in their body and brain, even though it ultimately has a negative effect.[29]

It may feel overwhelming to consider changing your eating habits, so know that starting small and with something manageable is okay. It may be as simple as eating a serving of vegetables or drinking eight glasses of water today. Small, healthy choices and changes can transform your nutrition habits, affecting not only how your body looks and feels but also how it heals from trauma over time.

I loved the feelings I experienced in the gym. I felt strong, hopeful, empowered, and capable of making change. I created a structure in my life so that I could feel that way every day. A disciplined schedule allowed me to function, build relationships, and focus as I got older so I could start building a business and a successful career.

Having a schedule gave me a sense of control over my life when things felt out of control. Living by a daily schedule turned out to be an effective emotional regulator. The sense of order, regularity, and predictability made me feel safe.

Dr. Bruce Perry, a neuroscientist who specializes in trauma treatment, describes what I call "a schedule" as "establishing a rhythm." It is one of the early interventions he encourages for those in overwhelmed emotional states, like I was. The brain needs a rhythm to help bring order when a tsunami of emotion could sink us. I established that in my life by establishing a daily schedule at the gym.[30]

That discipline in the gym was a major player that poured over into other aspects of my life. It gave me a sense of autonomy that enabled me to build a successful business and create a healthy life.

I didn't know *why* what I was doing was helping; all I knew was that this lifestyle made me want to live. It made me feel like I had purpose and value. It would take decades to start to understand how impactful it was that I leaned into this lifestyle rather than choosing drugs, alcohol, pornography, or suicide. I could have easily picked a coping mechanism that led me down a path of destruction and broken relationships and may have even led to me taking my own life.

I'm eternally grateful that this path presented itself, and it's the one I followed. But I know there are a lot of men and women out there who went through tragic things in their lives and, in the face of that internal pain, found solace and comfort in the drugs or alcohol that numbed those feelings. If you're one of those people, or if you love someone who is, I just want to say: There *is* hope. There is help. And there is a way back to a healthy, purposeful life.

EXPERT INSIGHTS:

Dr. Robert Rhoton: PsyD, LPC, FAAETS
Founder and Chief Clinical Officer, Arizona Trauma Institute

After years of working closely with people who've experienced trauma, one pattern has become strikingly clear: Trauma doesn't just leave emotional scars; it can deeply affect the body too.

Many survivors face long-term physical challenges, including digestive issues, chronic illness, and nutritional imbalances. That's because trauma disrupts how the brain and body communicate, particularly in areas like the diencephalon, a region of the brain whose structures include the thalamus and hypothalamus, which are deeply impacted by traumatic stress responses in the body. This overactivation of the diencephalon can lead to digestive issues, sleep disturbances, and lasting difficulties with emotional regulation, stress tolerance, and cognitive processing. As a result, people often develop disordered eating patterns—bingeing, emotional eating, or losing interest in food altogether. They may also turn to sugary, processed foods for comfort, which offer short-term relief but lead to long-term health risks like obesity and metabolic syndrome.[31]

But it goes even deeper. Trauma can trigger widespread inflammation, shift gut health, and throw off the body's ability to process nutrients. Many trauma survivors struggle with conditions like insulin resistance and nutrient deficiencies without realizing these symptoms are rooted in their trauma history.[32] Healing, then, is not just about therapy—it is about nourishing the body in a way that supports the mind too.

When nutrition and wellness are part of the recovery journey, people don't just heal—they begin to thrive. That's what Micah instinctively understood. His statement that our body *is* indeed a pharmacy is spot-on and scientifically validated. He was divinely inspired to understand that our body is a living system, perfectly created, that works in harmony through a highly complex network of chemical processes. As he said in this chapter, exercise is not enough. It needs to be supplemented with various other disciplined factors, such as nutrition and emotional regulation.

It starts in the body. When someone experiences trauma, it does not just live in their memories—it reshapes how their brain and body function. Stress hormones like cortisol often surge, while key neurotransmitters fall out of balance. That is why so many trauma survivors deal with fatigue, mood swings, and brain fog. That is also why Micah points out that his story could have easily taken a different path—one marked by drugs, alcohol, pornography, or even thoughts of suicide. These are not uncommon roads for people who have been through trauma; they are coping mechanisms that, while harmful, often begin as ways to manage overwhelming pain. There is no shame in that. When we are hurting, we all find ways—sometimes messy, sometimes quiet—to survive.

But here is the good news: Food can help. Whole, nourishing meals—with lean proteins, healthy fats, and complex carbs—can begin to gently rebalance those systems and support healing from the inside out.[33]

Certain nutrients play a starring role in recovery. Omega-3s (from fish, flaxseeds, or walnuts) help calm inflammation and boost the brain's ability to adapt and heal. B vitamins, like B6, B12, and folate, are essential for mood and mental clarity. Magnesium helps quiet the nervous system and improves sleep, while antioxidants in fruits and veggies help the body fight the stress damage trauma leaves behind.[34] And it is not just about the brain—the gut plays a huge part too. The gut and brain are constantly talking, and a healthy gut, fueled by probiotics (like yogurt and fermented foods) and prebiotics (like garlic and onions), can improve mood and resilience.[35]

Healing also calls for more than food.

Movement—whether it is a long walk, a stretching session, or dancing in your kitchen—helps release tension and lift your mood.[36] Mindfulness and meditation can quiet the brain's alarm system, helping you feel more grounded and in control.[37] And sleep—true, restful sleep—is vital. Simple changes like setting a bedtime routine or unplugging from screens can help your body rest and reset.

Ultimately, combining nutrition and wellness practices offers a powerful way to reclaim balance and well-being. Trauma may shape our physiology, but with the right care, healing and thriving are absolutely within reach.

Dr. Robert Rhoton
Arizona Trauma Institute, **www.AZtrauma.org**

39

STEP THREE: SECURING SAFETY

Diana's a great listener.

If you've ever had a chat with her, you know what I mean. She will look you straight in the eye like she's trying to see something deeper, she will lean in, and she will do her best to stay focused on what you're saying. One of her greatest gifts is the ability to really *see* people and make them feel seen. She excels at creating safe spaces for others, and she does it astoundingly quickly.

When I look back on our early conversations, she listened intently. Her focus was on me as I shared my story. Even though I had only known her briefly, I felt compassion, empathy, and respect from her. She made me feel safe. Since I knew she was a safe person, I shared openly.

The gym and my disciplined daily routine also created feelings of safety.

When Diana moved to Kansas City, we started our lives together and created an emotionally safe home. Even in the face of challenges, there was an underlying calm and peace.

Sharing my story with her early on was a big reason our relationship flourished. We had mutual trust and respect. We were committed to each other and built healthy boundaries to protect it. We shared open and honest communication about the things we had gone through in our lives, how they made us feel, and how they continued to impact us. I was also able to release all the fears of her thinking I was weak or less of a man because of what I had gone through.

I want to emphasize that I had to speak up and share with her. If I hadn't done that, there would still be this underlying, untold secret in our relationship. I know that a lot of men don't tell anyone, not even their spouses, not even if their spouse is a safe person.

I've heard from men who, after years of marriage, have finally shared that they feared being seen differently. They feared their wife would think they were weak or view them as damaged goods. I know that these fears hold true for both men and women, but perhaps even more powerfully for a man who feels the weight of shame from his abuse and fears that it made him less of a man.

If you have a loving spouse, someone you know is safe, but you've been afraid to share what you've gone through with them, I encourage you to take steps toward doing so. Maybe that's with or through a counselor or a pastor, or maybe it's just asking for a heart-to-heart conversation. Holding that in from the person that you have made a lifetime commitment to is carrying a burden and creating a wall in your relationship that you may not even realize.

If *you* are the spouse, and you suspect your partner has gone through abuse, but they won't let you in—or if they let you in, but it's years later, and you wonder why they waited so long—just know that *it wasn't you*. Everyone's healing journey looks different. You may provide the safest, most loving environment possible; you may be the best listener and emotionally sound; but that doesn't necessarily mean your partner will open up as quickly as I did.

Safety was critical for my journey, as it will be critical to anyone who has gone through abuse. Creating a safe environment with safe people and establishing boundaries against unsafe people and places has enabled me to heal from trauma and live a successful life.

For trauma survivors, your environment is going to have a massive impact on your healing process and how much you're able to heal.

Being in an unsafe environment or with unsafe people can very likely cause triggered responses and lead to retraumatization. Triggers are any stimuli that create an emotional response to danger in your body. Being constantly triggered won't create an environment where you can heal.

Here's what several studies regarding the importance of safety after traumatic experiences had to say:

> Feelings of safety may be fundamental in turning off the stress response. Failure to achieve feelings of safety, possibly owing to dysfunction of neuronal circuits that permit feelings of danger to abate, has been associated with the development of anxiety-related disorders.[38]

> When a stressor situation is one that does not permit feelings of safety to emerge, the activity of the anterior insula and amygdala are elevated.[39]

> The elevated neuronal activity at these sites may reflect continued efforts by the brain to make sense of the situation. It has indeed been suggested that safety may be a learned response that fosters feelings of security and protection, but if safety is not established features of pathology (e.g., hypervigilance associated with PTSD) may evolve.[40]

Safety is necessary for healing; unsafety will likely lead to even more problems in the future.

Here are six ideas for building a physically and psychologically safe environment in your home:

1. *Listen to your partner.* We live in a distracted world, so make sure you create space in your relationship for uninterrupted, focused communication. Make them feel seen and heard. Don't try to fix or solve it in that moment. Don't even tell them, "Everything is going to be okay." First, just listen, be present in the pain, and hold it with them in that space.
2. *Be kind.* If you are living with a spouse who has gone through abuse, be patient and kind if they are working through their healing journey. Some of it may not make sense to you. If you are the survivor, do your best to be kind and gracious to your spouse as well, since they might not quite understand how your brain is wired.
3. *Be clear and transparent.* If you are revealing the abuse, don't try to hide what you're feeling or isolate yourself when you're struggling. Let your partner in as much as you can (and this may take time). Let them be a part of the healing journey.
4. *Be calm.* For both of you, when conflict arises, learn the necessary tools and skills (these are called self-regulation skills) to calm down before you start a battle with your spouse. There are many self-regulation techniques that can help bring the temperature of the conversation down a notch.[41] It's best when this goes both ways, but you only have control over yourself, so learn it first and model it for your partner. Conflict needs to be resolved, but yelling, screaming, and name-calling do not create a space conducive to effective communication. Getting your body regulated (aka calm) will be far more productive for the results and resolution both of you are seeking.

5. *Set boundaries.* This is important for relationships and individuals. Clear boundaries protect a relationship from outside threats. Setting individual boundaries (which may mean giving space for self-care) and respecting those will help build trust and safety in a relationship.
6. *Seek counseling.* We aren't all master communicators, and processing complex human emotions isn't easy! There's no shame in seeking counseling to help you understand your spouse and work together to build a safe environment where you can both thrive.

EXPERT INSIGHTS:

Candice Raine: PC, ACC, TRLC
CEO, Arizona Trauma Institute

Childhood Sexual Abuse (CSA) disrupts a child's foundational sense of safety, security, and trust, with long-lasting consequences for adult relationships and emotional regulation. Scientific research strongly supports this, particularly in the domains of trust, vulnerability, attachment, and social connection.

Safety has multiple dimensions: physical, emotional, psychological, relational, and spiritual. All are foundational to trauma recovery because they create the conditions necessary for healing, resilience, and the restoration of well-being.

What Micah is referring to in this chapter is emotional, psychological, and relational safety. In order to reach a point where he could trust, Micah had to overcome a major burden. He had to break the chains that kept him tied to a constant sense of imminent danger, hence the panic attacks he refers to in an earlier part of the book. Micah, through intense self-reflective work and through his faith, reopened the door to being openly vulnerable to others, thus developing trust in sharing his story.

However, trust does not happen overnight. When Micah was experiencing all this validation from his environment as a result of being a successful fitness model, he was displaying an "external locus of control," meaning that he was attributing success or failure to factors outside his personal control (i.e., other people's validation). When Micah made this realization, he might not have fully appreciated the magnitude of this step in his recovery. Developing an "internal locus of control" means that he recognized that the outcomes of his life are influenced by his own efforts, decisions, and abilities. This is like screaming from the rooftops, "I am worthy!" Research shows that the presence of an internal locus of control is a positive factor for mental health and self-esteem in recovery.[42]

Micah's ability to interpret Diana's response to his experience as caring and selfless is an indication of his growth and recovery. Disclosure in a safe environment is a critical and essential aspect of recovery.[43] By creating this support system around him, Micah established a foundational environment fostering his ongoing recovery.

I am a survivor myself and have been in active recovery for several years. To this day, creating a safe environment is something that I have made a critical part of my life. It will look different for everybody. For Micah, in addition to his relationship with Diana, it is about a network of close friends whom he entrusts to accompany him through some of the most difficult steps of his healing, such as joining him at the court where he testified. It also means the gym, where he connects with his body and allows himself to feel—something that many survivors have a very difficult time doing. Lastly, and most importantly, his relationship with Christ represents a foundational source of safety.

For me, it means wrapping myself in a warm blanket and being surrounded by my pets. It means going on a road trip with my husband. It means watching a movie with my son. More recently, committing my life to our Savior and putting God first has had a profound impact on my ability to feel safe.

Candice Raine
CEO, Arizona Trauma Institute
www.AZtrauma.org

40

STEP FOUR: RESTORING FAITH

My relationship with Jesus was hijacked.

Kenny was a man filled with perverse, selfish ambition and sexual urges he was determined to fulfill, no matter who it hurt or at what cost it came.

I shudder to think how many more victims there were. Kenny worked with children his entire life. He sought out situations where he had access, places where he could easily spot his prey. He worked in preschools, drove a bus for children with special needs, and even led church youth activities. How many more are there like me but who are holding that pain in silence? Whose lives were destroyed because of this monster who have chosen paths that are alternate to mine? How many battle addiction? How many struggle with guilt, shame, embarrassment, depression, anxiety, or anger, and never get the help they need? Perhaps some of them took their own lives. These are all questions I'll never know the answer to, but there are times that I wonder about them and pray for them, hoping they are alright.

Kenny fed me a warped version of God, one who excused his behavior, confusing me until I couldn't tell the real Jesus from the counterfeit.

When he used faith as a means of manipulating me to satisfy his lustful sickness, it wasn't just physical; it was spiritual abuse that marred my view of God.

When people hear how faith was twisted to hurt me, they are often stunned that I turned my heart and my life back to Jesus. Abuse in the church has turned countless individuals away from God. And that makes sense. I was one of them.

I wanted nothing to do with the church after my abuse. Kenny wasn't just a church member; he was one of their leaders. He was elevated as someone to look up to and emulate; they gave him a position of authority that allowed him even more access to kids like me. The younger me cringed at that thought. Why would I ever want to go to a church with a bunch of people talking about God and how much they love Him, but they either are doing horrible things in their lives or are promoting people who are abusing kids behind closed doors? How did they not know what was going on? So as far as the church goes, it was a *nope, not for me.*

When someone uses religious beliefs to hurt, manipulate, or control you—such as how Kenny taught me that God *wanted* him to abuse me—it leaves a deep spiritual wound, one that can't be seen. But if left unhealed, it inflicts damage and bondage that will impact every aspect of life.

I was angry at God for a long time. I was confused. I thought I was a good kid. Was God even real? Was He even there? In the midst of the abuse, I cried out to Him to protect me, but the abuse didn't stop. Maybe I was a bad kid after all. But what had I done so wrong to deserve this?

I couldn't make it make sense.

Diana's question that day in Las Vegas stopped me cold: "Why were you mad at God?" That's when I started digging. The answers didn't come as a clear "why"—they unfolded slowly as I searched for "who" He was.

I brought my pain and frustration directly to Him, and I let Him know that I was angry. And to my surprise, He was okay with that. He let me vent my pain, and as I started opening my heart back up to a relationship with Him, I realized that He was grieving and angry about Kenny's choices too. As I poured my heart out, I felt Him comforting me, not condemning me.

My path to a relationship with Him was a gentle journey where I discovered the loving Father that I had always longed for, who would never and had never abused or forsaken me.

I realized God isn't a puppet master; Kenny chose evil with his own free will, not because God willed it.

I learned that even when we go through the most horrific storms and unbearable traumas, Jesus is there to comfort us when we cry, strengthen us when we are weak, and hold us when we feel like we can no longer hold on.

I also had to reconcile with my church hurt.

Kenny was a master manipulator. The people at church couldn't see through his religious mask. Most predators lurking in churches don't have a criminal record since most victims remain silent, and abuse is often by a family member or someone close to the family. It's a problem in the church that isn't limited to one specific denomination. I hope this book sparks conversation around that topic as well so that, collectively, we can find ways to protect more kids from predators who use the church as a hunting ground.

For years, that betrayal kept me from God and His people. But as I started trusting Jesus again, letting Him into my anger, I saw Kenny's lies for what they were: a distortion, not the truth. That shifted everything. Once my relationship with Jesus was solid, I could look at church differently, not as a den of hypocrites but as a messy family of broken folks like me.

I must be so clear about the importance of my faith being restored. This rebuilt my foundation—for every healing step after that, I leaned on God's strength.

I can't tell you my story authentically or help you understand how I've achieved a level of healing that is beyond the barrier of pain tolerance or pain management that most people hit without sharing these pieces with you too.

The reason I am strong enough in mind, body, and spirit to write this book and step into this next phase of life without fear and with breathless anticipation of what is in store for the impact and healing of others is Jesus.

I've got to give the credit where credit is due and point you to Him. Maybe you know Him, and maybe you don't; maybe you're curious about Him, and maybe you question if He even exists. Regardless, thank you for listening to my heart on this.

Without this crucial piece of the puzzle, my healing journey would have hit a brick wall. I'm not talking about "religion." So often, people hear me share my faith and think that I'm religious. That's not the case. I'm not chasing religion, made up of rules and boxes to check, but rather a real relationship with Jesus. That's what healed me, not a pew.

I'm not knocking going to church, either, so please hear my heart on this. Fellowship and community are *really* important. After I went through several steps of healing, I was ready to find a church family. Diana and I have grown so much through our pastor and this group of people who love us, encourage us, and grow with us. Coming together at church to worship God and build relationships that edify, and the opportunity to do life with those who share your faith, is an incredible gift when they are safe people.

If you were hurt in church or by someone who was "religious," then the thought of going to church as part of healing may be triggering for you. Let me assure you that you don't have to set foot inside a church to find healing. Yet as you heal, you'll see that the person who hurt you didn't speak for God; they defied Him, and *that* understanding can open the door for you to find a safe community of believers when you're ready.

If someone asked me how I built my physique, I wouldn't tell them that it was the result of years of discipline, healthy eating, and exercise but that they could instead be undisciplined, eat junk food, not work out, and still achieve the same result. No way. I would be specific about *exactly* what was needed to achieve the goal.

I feel the same way about my faith, and that's why I'm bold about it.

It's my relationship with Jesus that fills me with love. It's why I can love people regardless of where they are in life or what their faith journey is. It's His love that overflows through me and makes all that possible. I couldn't have done that in my own strength.

How did I get there?

One prayer, one conversation, one step of faith at a time.

I slowly started to trust Jesus.

Like anyone else in my life whom I've trusted, I had to get to know them and find out about their character.

I started talking to Him and learning about Him. The more I leaned into my relationship with Him through prayer, reading the Bible, and eventually finding a church home, the more I understood how much He loved me and how much He hated what happened to me too.

Through my pain, when I cried out to Him, I recall many times when I felt Him saying, *Hold on, I have something for you.* It didn't make sense then, but now I know: God didn't do this to me. A man consumed with evil in his life did this to me. The devil wanted to destroy me, but there's a verse in the Bible, Genesis 50:20, that says, "You intended to harm me, but God intended it for good to accomplish what is now being done, the saving of many lives."[44]

As I turned my eyes back to the Lord, I began to understand. He was with me, and He was going to turn these horrible circumstances, all my pain, into strength. I would be stronger than ever so that I could help others who have gone through something similar. He would use me to help others break free.

Building a relationship with Jesus is just like building a friendship. You meet some people, and they become acquaintances. You may know their name and say hello here and there, but you don't really know them. You aren't aware of what is happening in their lives. You don't know their heart and character. In true friendship, you get to know that person. You share about yourself and let them in; you ask questions, listen to them, and get to know their heart. You *know* them.

That's how my faith has grown. I know a lot of men and women who have turned their hearts away from the Lord because they were abused by someone in the church or someone claiming to be a person of faith. The hijacked version of "faith" that they were shown has hardened their hearts to the true heart and nature of God.

I get it. I did the same thing for a season. I had to muster the courage to go back and reevaluate what I had been taught.

I discovered that some people speak and use Jesus' name but don't know Him. Even worse, they may be using His name as a means of manipulation to gain an opportunity to abuse. It may look as if many of those abusers get away with it, but there will be consequences for them. I will leave it at that.

Throughout my faith journey with Jesus, I've become a different person.

I used to be filled with anxiety and stress, much of it stemming from abuse, but now I have an internal peace. It's constant and doesn't fluctuate depending on the circumstances I'm facing. Most people think that peace is the absence of conflict. We have peace when there is no war raging, right? But that's not real peace. That's being calm when the waters are calm, and no challenges are being faced. But *real* peace is unchanging, no matter what is happening around you. Real peace is a person. It's Jesus.

It's an amazing thing to have peace, even through the greatest challenges that life has thrown my way.

Another remarkable change that has happened within me is the shift from pursuing feelings of *happiness* to experiencing a constant underlying *joy*.

I used to chase after happy feelings, and as soon as the feeling diminished, I'd start looking for the next hit of happiness. The gym was a huge part of that for me. I got that dopamine rush that made me feel good, so I kept going, again and again. When things seemed good in life, I felt happy. But when a challenge came or something bad happened, I plunged right back into unhappiness, or even despair and depression at times.

And yes, I still work out because I love how it makes me feel, and I am a happy guy right after a workout; there's no doubt about it. But I have something even more profound now too. Happiness fades with circumstances, but joy, like peace, stays constant, a gift from God.

Chasing happiness seems to be the name of the game nowadays, with everyone looking for what they can "do" to be happy or feel happy. There's nothing wrong with most of those pursuits, and it's great to feel happy. But joy is deeper.

People often tell me that I'm a happy guy. And they aren't wrong—I am happy most of the time. You can ask Diana too. I love mornings; I wake up at 3:00 a.m. every day, like clockwork. I have a morning routine that I love. I spend time in prayer, I read the Bible, I do cardio for one to two hours (just slow cardio; I get my social media work done during this time), and I listen to worship music. By the time she gets up a couple of hours later, I am on a happiness high! I'm full of energy and excitement for the day, and I let her know it. My wife, being a slow riser and a quiet morning person, often just stares at me, letting me know it's not yet time for words.

But beyond the happiness, I've got joy.

When I think about my life had I not turned my eyes and heart back to the Lord, I don't know where I would be today. I would still have a successful business and a high level of fitness. But big pieces would be missing. My marriage would not be the same, my outlook on life would not be the same, and my healing journey would not be as complete. I seriously doubt if this book would have ever come to fruition or if I would have reached the point where I could share my story openly. I can't imagine having the strength on my own to turn from the shame that gripped me. Nor would I have the same message of hope to offer others.

There's one thing I know for certain: Without Jesus, I'd still be stuck—no peace, no joy. If my faith had not been restored, I wouldn't have been able to move on to the next step of my healing journey. Which was the hardest one to take. Forgiveness.

EXPERT INSIGHTS:

Bryan Vignery, Licensed Clinical Professional Counselor

It's pretty natural for us to want to blame a perfect God when bad things happen, especially when the person who wronged us holds a position of spiritual authority. This is exactly what the enemy wants—to twist our view of God, whether through small or overwhelming traumas.

In Romans, Paul told us, "And we know that God causes everything to work together for the good of those who love God and are called according to his purpose for them" (Romans 8:28 NLT).

We're all designed with a purpose, one that God has planted in us, aiming to shape us into the likeness of Jesus.

Once we truly recognize that God is a loving, caring Father, our life's purpose starts to come into focus. God uses every circumstance to work for the good of those who love Him. I've seen this truth play out time and again in people's lives. The struggle to fully trust God, to wrestle with Him, is often the very journey He leads us on. It's through this process that we're equipped to help others see His truth.

So, think of it this way: Even in our darkest moments, God is crafting a story in which our pain can lead to purpose, not just for us but also for others. It's a messy, beautiful journey toward trust, healing, and, ultimately, a deeper connection with God.

Bryan Vignery, LCPC
https://www.intentionalway.com

41
STEP FIVE: FORGIVENESS

Forgiveness was one of the most challenging pieces of the healing puzzle for me. Throughout my story in this book I have shared hints of how I got to that point, but now I'd like to take a deeper dive.

I know that the concept of forgiveness may sound absurd and unobtainable if you've gone through abuse yourself. If you're not there yet, I get it. This took years for me and was not an easy process. But it's a release that has enabled a complete rewiring of my mind. It's the step that truly shifted me from a victim to a victor.

In the world's eyes, it is acceptable to go through life without ever forgiving. It is considered normal to hold on to anger and a desire for revenge. At the thought of offering forgiveness for something horrible that's happened to you at the hands of another, you may say, "That's fine for you, but you don't know what happened to me."

And you're right, I don't know your story, and you do not have to forgive. Forgiveness is your choice. Unforgiveness is also a choice. Either path produces a result in your life. I'd like to share a bit about those two paths, and you can choose what's best for you.

One thing I've learned is that unforgiveness doesn't hurt the other person; it just festers in me, growing roots of bitterness that can choke the goodness out of my life.

There's a famous quote attributed to multiple people that sums up the result of unforgiveness: "It's like drinking poison and expecting the other person to die."

Unforgiveness destroys you from the inside out, allowing anger, resentment, bitterness, and hatred to infiltrate all aspects of your life.

Forgiveness, on the other hand, opened a door to peace in my life that I didn't know existed.

To be clear, forgiveness doesn't mean that what was done to me wasn't pure evil, or that I should have a relationship with Kenny, or that he should ever be trusted around children, or shouldn't suffer consequences for his actions.

Forgiveness in the heart is simply releasing that person from control over me. It's viewing them through a different lens and seeing how broken they truly are. As far as Kenny is concerned, I started to see that he wasn't just my abuser; he was a victim too. You see, he was sexually abused as a boy. Something in him twisted that pain into power over others. He chose to carry that abuse forward and destroy the lives of Lord knows how many boys. He never went through healing. Instead, he coped with his trauma and the sickness it created in him by hurting others. He chose a life of bondage to sin.

How did I get to this point? It's hard to imagine, after all I've shared, that I can write these words, telling you that in my heart, I've forgiven the man who abused me and many others, stole my childhood, and stole my innocence.

I wrestled with this for decades.

I recognized when I was preparing to share my story for the first time on stage, and then again when I went through the trial process, that I had released Kenny and forgiven him.

I was able to reach that point of forgiving because I started to really understand what Jesus did for me on the cross.

Let me explain.

Jesus was murdered in the most horrific way known to man at that time, crucifixion. He was placed on a cross in front of His mother, along with His friends and enemies. What you may not think about when it comes to this story is that Jesus was naked. When you see pictures of Him on the cross, He is typically covered up, so when we hear this story, we don't often picture Him this way.

But there wouldn't be any clothing. Jesus would have been totally exposed and humiliated. Exposure is a form of sexual abuse. He suffered in this humiliating fashion, paying the price for the sins of the world for those who come to Him in repentance. That means for my sin, for Kenny's sin if he truly repented from it, and for your sin if you bring it to the cross.

And what did Jesus do in that moment of horror, in that moment of shame, in that moment of absolute torture and humiliation? What were His words?

"Father, forgive them, for they know not what they do" (Luke 23:34).[45]

Jesus prayed for forgiveness for His abusers *while* He was being crucified.

Wow.

That hit me hard. If I want to be more like Jesus, I have to forgive. I chose to forgive Kenny, I chose to forgive my mom, and I even chose to forgive myself. If Jesus did it, that means He would give me the strength to do it too.

EXPERT INSIGHTS:

Brent Stromme
Pastor, professional speaker, and life coach

Reading Micah's story, you immediately feel the weight of the battle he fought—and the depth of the healing he has found.

Forgiveness, in his journey, was not about minimizing the evil done to him. It wasn't about pretending the pain didn't matter. It was about freeing himself from being forever chained to the hurt. Choosing to forgive freed Micah to move forward, releasing him from living constantly in reaction to his pain. It cut the tie between his identity and the evil done to him.

Forgiveness didn't excuse the actions of those who caused or added to his pain; it didn't erase the consequences. But it unlocked the door to a new kind of life—a life of freedom, no longer ruled by bitterness, anger, or revenge.

Micah's healing journey shows that forgiveness is an act of obedience to God, a gift He offers to us, and a gift we choose to give ourselves. It is the refusal to allow the wounds inflicted by others to define us any longer. It is choosing life over death, hope over despair, freedom over bondage.

Healing is one of the most powerful forces in the world because it reflects the very heart of God. Healing is not just about feeling better—it's about being restored. It's about moving from brokenness to wholeness.

In Scripture, God repeatedly reveals Himself as a healer: "He heals the brokenhearted and binds up their wounds" (Psalm 147:3).[46]

"'But I will restore you to health and heal your wounds,' declares the LORD" (Jeremiah 30:17).[47]

Jesus said, "It is not the healthy who need a doctor, but the sick" (Luke 5:31).[48]

God does not minimize our pain. He acknowledges it, steps into it, and offers us a way through it. Healing is a core part of His character because He is a Redeemer—He takes what was meant for evil and turns it for good (Genesis 50:20). When Micah chose to forgive, he aligned his heart with God's greater story: that evil would not have the final word. Love would.

Forgiveness draws us into the very heartbeat of God, who does not hold our sins against us. He promises to remember them no more (Hebrews 8:12) and to remove them from us as far as the east is from the west (Psalm 103:12). His forgiveness is not cautious or reserved—it is complete, extravagant, overflowing, and free. When we choose to forgive, even when it hurts, we are stepping into that same wide, merciful grace—and learning to live unbound by the chains that once tried to hold us.

The power of healing is that it transforms not just how we live but how we love. A healed heart can love freely again, can dream again, can trust again—not because the world is suddenly safe or certain but because we are rooted in the unshakable love of God. Healing restores the ability to live in the present rather than being imprisoned by the past.

Ultimately, Micah's story reminds us that forgiveness is not something we muster up by sheer willpower. It is something we receive from God and pass along. We forgive because we are forgiven (Ephesians 4:32). We heal because the Healer lives within us. We love because He first loved us (1 John 4:19). And when we choose forgiveness, even when it feels impossible, we experience the resurrection life of Jesus right here, right now—turning graves into gardens, mourning into dancing, ashes into beauty.

Forgiveness is a hard road, and for many survivors of abuse, it can seem not just difficult but downright impossible. Micah's story doesn't diminish that reality—it honors it. But it also lights a candle of hope. Healing is possible. Freedom is possible. And it all begins with one courageous, grace-fueled choice: to forgive.

Reflection:

Where have you been carrying the weight of unforgiveness? Will you ask Jesus to show you the places He longs to heal in you and to help you trust Him with every wound?

Prayer:

Jesus, I give You my hurt, my anger, and my fear. Fill the empty places with Your healing love.
Teach me to forgive, not because it's easy but because You are with me—and You make all things new.

Brent Stromme
www.BrentStromme.com

42
STEP SIX: MESS TO MISSION

My life was a mess. Thankfully, messes can be cleaned up! But they don't clean themselves.

Even though there are so many parts of my mess that weren't of my doing, I had to take action and make movement to "clean it up," turning something chaotic, confusing, and destructive into something clear and purposeful. I turned my mess into my mission. The Breaker Mission.

I could have gone through this immense healing journey that I've shared with you and left it at that. That would have been incredible in itself—to live healed and with a healthy marriage and business. However, I would not have felt truly fulfilled in life or that I had completely said yes to God's calling, His invitation for my life, if I hadn't taken all the pain and turned it into something purposeful that would positively and powerfully impact others.

Although I thought I would never share about my abuse, I have no problem sharing about it now. Anytime I tell someone new, as I see them start sinking into sadness and grief for me (and I know for some of them it's pulling them into the grief of their own story too), I can't wait to get them through to the other side filled with hope. I feel like saying, "But wait . . . there's more!" as I unveil what God did for me.

My friend "Chill Bill" (from chapter 8) was one of my lifelines during my abuse, along with his family—even though he wasn't aware of what I was going through. He came to visit Diana and me in Kansas City recently. I hadn't seen him in person for over a decade because he was serving in the military and had moved to Texas.

For a couple of hours he shared about his military ventures, about his family, and about his walk with the Lord. We shared what was going on in our world a bit, and then Diana looked at me and said, "Okay, you need to tell him."

I started to share my story, opening up about the darkness and despair that had held me captive for so long. Bill broke down in tears as I spoke of the horror, shame, and depression that ensued. He shook his head and said, "I didn't know."

Diana sat there, fidgeting; she gets so excited for people to hear the end of the story and how it turns out, she has to physically contain herself from jumping in and saying, "Just wait till you hear what happens next!"

We finally reached the part of the story where I shared the impact that Bill's family had on me, how they had literally *saved* my life and given me hope. The tears from both of us were pouring out. Diana stood there with a little smile on her face as we embraced each other, and she snapped a photo of the moment. Bill was overwhelmed and overjoyed to know the role he had played in this "God story," and it was such a blessing for me to be able to share it with him. It felt like being able to give a gift to thank him for the priceless gift that he gave me.

I feel that way about The Breaker Mission. Jesus gave me a priceless gift, not just in His sacrifice as my Savior but in the freedom that

He's given me from chains that had me shackled for so long. John 8:36 says, "So if the Son sets you free, you will be free indeed."[49] I am a walking, talking testimony to that truth, and the best way that I know to thank Him for that gift is to share about it and spread this message of hope as far and wide as I possibly can.

"You are most powerfully positioned to serve the person you once were." I've heard that quote from multiple sources, including Rory Vaden, Brian Covey, and Ed Mylett.[50] It lands with me every time. I'm here to be a loud voice in a space where silence has suffocated so many men and women. Helping others break free from shame and the shackles of past trauma and abuse is how I will turn my greatest test into my greatest testimony. That's what I plan on doing, for as many days as the Lord gives me on this earth.

You've endured deep pain, as we all have. But no matter how overwhelming that pain feels or how daunting the healing journey seems, there is light waiting for you. There is hope. You were created for a purpose far greater than your struggles. The strength you've gained through survival, once healed, can become the very gift that uplifts and inspires others. You are not alone, and your story holds the power to change lives.

EXPERT INSIGHTS:

Psychoanalyst Jessica Almond

Some wounds are so deep they seem impossible to name. Buried beneath shame and fear, they do not disappear with time. Instead, they persist in the unconscious, shaping thoughts, emotions, and behaviors in ways that often go unnoticed—until they can no longer be ignored.

For many people who have experienced childhood sexual abuse, silence is more suffocating than the memories themselves. Confusion, guilt, and an unbearable fear of being seen as weak keep them from speaking out. For men, this silence is compounded by cultural expectations—strength, self-reliance, and control. But what happens when those very qualities feel lost in the wake of trauma?

People who have experienced abuse often feel a deep inner division: the self they present to the world (capable, strong, seemingly whole) and the self that carries the unbearable truth of what was done. This division is not a conscious choice but a survival mechanism. When the mind cannot make sense of betrayal, it splits.

This explains why many struggle with memories that feel distant or unreal, as though they belong to someone else. Trauma is stored not just in the mind but in the body, surfacing as tension, anxiety, or unexplained shame. It all lingers beneath the surface, waiting to be understood.

For those abused by someone they trusted, the betrayal is even more devastating. A child cannot comprehend how love and violence can come from the same source. Unable to process such contradictions, the child may take on the guilt themselves, believing on some level that they were responsible, that they should have stopped it, that they deserved it, or, worse, that they somehow allowed it to happen.

To cope, some bury themselves in achievement, control, or emotional detachment. Others turn to substances or self-destructive behaviors. But no matter how deeply trauma is buried, it inevitably finds its way to the surface through relationships, patterns of avoidance, or the quiet ache of isolation.

Micah's story illustrates these struggles. Throughout his adolescent years and young adulthood, he appeared confident and successful, yet privately he felt hollow and ashamed. His public persona was not just a social mask but an unconscious psychological defense—one that kept him from facing the full weight of his pain.

One of the greatest burdens people carry after abuse is the fear of being truly seen. They fear judgment, misunderstanding, or even rejection. For men, this fear is especially intense. Many believe admitting to victimization threatens their very identity. They worry that others will see them as weak or, worse, permanently damaged.

But secrecy does not erase pain; it deepens it. The more trauma is hidden, the more it festers. The mind constructs defenses—rationalization, avoidance, emotional numbness—but these eventually break down, often in unexpected and painful ways.

Micah's story shows how breaking the silence can be transformative. When he speaks out, others recognize their own struggles in his words. He discovered that healing is not a solitary journey but one that requires connection.

Healing is not about erasing the past but reclaiming power in the present. The first step is to name the experience and allow the truth to exist without shame. What happened was not a reflection of one's worth, masculinity, or strength. It was a violation, not a definition of self.

The second step is understanding that trauma is not something one can "think" their way out of. It is stored in the nervous system, in the body's very response to the world. Healing requires relationships—safe, attuned connections that allow people to relearn what safety feels like.

Many people fear that trust is dangerous, that betrayal will repeat itself. But in the right relationships, new experiences take root. There is no undoing the past, but there is the possibility of rewriting how it shapes the present.

The final step is transformation. Many fear that acknowledging their past will consume them. But the truth is that the only way out is through. When trauma is finally brought into the light, it loses its power.

Healing does not mean forgetting. It means integrating and allowing the past to exist without being controlled by it. For those who choose to share their story, healing takes on an even greater purpose. When one person speaks, they create space for others to do the same.

For Micah, healing meant confronting how trauma shaped his relationships, his sense of self-worth, and his body. He realized true strength lay not in avoidance but in vulnerability and connection. Over time, his trauma became the catalyst for growth. He helps others, creating spaces where men can share their stories and reclaim their lives.

For those still trapped in silence, know this: The pain you carry is not yours to bear alone. There is no shame in what was done to you, only in the secrecy that keeps you from healing. You were never weak for surviving. And you are not weak for wanting more than survival—you are strong enough to reclaim your life.

Jessica Almond, LPC, LCPC
Professional Counselor-Psychoanalyst
www.jessicaalmond.com

EPILOGUE

THE ONE

Are you still here? Great, I hoped you'd stick around just a little longer. If you're reading this now, then you're "the One."

You're the guy I wrote this book for. You stuck with me through the worst of my story—the pain, the shame, the darkness—and you saw me come out the other side, free. I know it's been heavy at times. Thank you for carrying the weight with me.

I want to talk to you for a minute, just you and me, man to man. You're not just reading a story anymore; I'm inviting you into one.

A while back, my friend Luke Askew from the UK shared a vision he had that stuck with me. He saw me in a room, a safe place, something that looked like a podcast studio. One by one, guys walked in. Not a crowd, just one at a time. I'd listen to their stories, share mine, and help them start breaking free from the shame, guilt, or pain they were carrying. Diana was there, just outside the door, making the space feel solid, like you could let your guard down without worrying. Luke told me the message was to keep my focus on "the One" God brings me each day. After hearing this, it became my prayer: "Lord, send me 'the One' today."

God answers that prayer all the time. I meet "the One" at the grocery store, the gym, or one of our SoulFIT retreats. Some share my faith; others don't. Some have been through abuse like me; others have different wounds. But the pain cuts just as deep either way. Some have never shared their story with anyone, and I'm the first person they trust. Others have shared their experiences before but never found someone who truly understands.

Then there are the guys who've hurt others, maybe because their own pain was never dealt with. If that's you, if you're carrying the weight of hurting someone else, this is for you too. Hurt people hurt people, but healed people can heal people. You're not too far gone.

You've read my story. You know it didn't end with me stuck in pain. I didn't just figure out how to deal with the shame or live with the wounds. I fought my way to freedom, and I'm living it now. Maybe you're reading this and thinking, *That's great for you, Micah, but I can't see that happening for me.* Maybe freedom feels like a long shot, like you're too deep in the muck to ever get out. I hear you. I was there too, drowning in silence, thinking the pain would own me forever. But I'm telling you, freedom is real, and it's for you too. You're not meant to stay in that darkness. You can break through, just like I did.

I invite you to picture the space that Luke envisioned. It's your turn to come on in. The door opens, and Diana greets you with a big smile, leading you in to meet me. We shake hands and have a seat. It's just you and me, sitting across from each other in a simple room, nothing fancy, just a place where you can be real. I'm looking at you, not judging, just ready to listen. I see the burden you're carrying, the stuff you've never told anyone, the pain or guilt that's been eating at you. I'm not here to fix you or push you. I'm just a guy who's been through the fire, ready to hear you out, because I know what it's like to carry that kind of weight. This is your moment to lay it down.

Let me tell you something straight up: You are not your pain. You are not the lies you believed to keep going. You are not the shame or the secrets. You are not what was done to you, and you are not what you've done. You are worth fighting for. You are worth healing. You're not in this alone.

There's someone who's been with you every step, even when you didn't feel Him. His name is Jesus. Maybe you know Him, maybe you don't, or maybe your relationship with Him got messed up because of church hurt or people who let you down. I get it. I was angry at God for a long time too. But Jesus isn't scared of your pain or your past. He's the Breaker, the One who goes first and breaks the chains so you can break through after Him and claim the freedom that is rightfully yours. If you're curious about Him or want to get to know Him, just let me know. I'd love to introduce you.

He showed up in my darkest moments and said, "Hold on, I've got something for you." I'm telling you the same thing now. Hold on. You don't have to wear a mask, you don't have to pretend it's fine, you don't have to keep living with the shame, guilt, pain, anger, addictions, fear, or insecurities any longer.

I won't lie and tell you this is easy. It's not. Just like any superhero, the journey to get your cape is loaded with challenges, obstacles, fights, and enemies that seem to increase in size as you progress. But I promise you, if you're willing to step in, do the work, tap into the strength that's in you, and courageously face the monsters, it's worth every ounce of effort. The man you are destined to become, the strongest, healthiest, healed, purpose-filled version of you, is waiting on the other side of the battle.

I want to hear your story. Not the one you tell to keep people off your back, or the one you share to prove yourself to the world. I want to hear the real one. The one you've been carrying for too long on your own.

I'm listening . . .

And in the meantime, let me leave you with one more thought: I'm sorry for what you've gone through. It's hard. It matters. You matter. This isn't the end. It's the start of your freedom. It's time for you to become a Breaker.

I'm here for you, brother. Let's do this.

Micah

P.S. Meet up with me now at www.thebreakermission.com. I've created a space where you can write me directly to share your story, doubts, fears, victories, or the impact this book has had on you. Can't wait to hear from you!

RESOURCES

These resources are curated to support your journey through trauma, shame, and healing, with a focus on faith, strength, and community. Whether you are a survivor, a supporter, or are seeking to grow, these tools can help you break through to freedom.

Organizations

- **RAINN (Rape, Abuse and Incest National Network)**
  www.rainn.org
- **1in6**
  www.1in6.org
- **The Forge (Iron Sharpens Iron)**
  www.ironsharpensiron.net
- **Pure Life Ministries**
  www.purelifeministries.org
- **Freedom Academy**
  www.wearefm.org

Faith-Based Healing Books

- *Free & Fully Alive* by Karrie Garcia
- *The Wounded Heart: Hope for Adult Victims of Childhood Sexual Abuse* by Dan B. Allender

- ***Mending the Soul: Understanding and Healing Abuse*** by Steven R. Tracy

Fitness Programs for Mind, Body, and Spirit

- **Hitch Fit**
  Founded by Micah and Diana LaCerte, Hitch Fit offers online and in-person fitness coaching. It blends physical training with faith-based encouragement to transform body, mind, and spirit.
  www.hitchfit.com
- **SoulFIT Retreats**
  SoulFIT Retreats combine faith, fitness, and personal growth in transformative events. These retreats foster community and spiritual strength, empowering you to live with purpose.
  www.soulfitretreats.com

Expert Contributors

These experts contributed to *The Breaker*, offering faith-based and trauma-informed guidance. Visit their websites for coaching, workshops, or resources.

- **Bryan Vignery**
  www.intentionalway.com
- **Jessica Almond**
  www.jessicaalmond.com
- **Brent Stromme**
  www.brentstromme.com
- **Candice Raine**
  www.aztrauma.org
- **Dr. Bob Rhoton**
  www.aztrauma.org

ACKNOWLEDGMENTS

All honor and gratitude to my Lord and Savior, Jesus Christ—The Breaker.

He is the reason I am standing here today.

His love brought me back to life. His truth shattered the chains of shame, fear, and silence that once held me captive. Without Him, I would still be bound. Without Him, I would not have found full freedom.

Every breakthrough I have experienced—every moment of healing, every word in this book—is because of Him.

This is not just my story.

This is His redemption written through me.

Thank You, Jesus.

To my wife, Diana, what an incredible blessing you are.

You did not just write this book . . . you helped restore the man behind it. From the beginning, you gave me something I had never truly known—a safe place to fully heal and a foundation built on Christ. With you, I did not have to carry the weight alone or pretend to have it all together. And in that space, I finally had room to open up, to get vulnerable, to face my past, and to begin walking in true freedom.

You were the one who brought my story to life through your writing. God gave you a powerful gift to use for a greater purpose.

You saw the broken child inside me that needed healing. You saw what was buried beneath the trauma. You saw the man I could be. You were with me in the valley when it was hard, when it was heavy, and when it felt impossible.

You carried my pain like it was your own, and you turned it into something beautiful that now has the power to help others step out of the darkness and into healing.

There is no part of this healing, this mission, or this message that exists without you.

I love you forever.

To my parents and family—

Thank you for loving me through it all. Your prayers and support gave me the foundation I needed to rise.

To my father—you are a ROCKSTAR with a beautiful caring heart. Thank you.

To my mother—

Through all the pain, you have continued to press forward. And while the road has not always been easy, there were many beautiful moments that left a lasting impact and helped shape the good in me. Thank you for never giving up.

To the friends who became like family—

God blessed me with some of the most amazing people in the world. Nolan Brown, Bill Meisenzahl and his wonderful family, Adam Gross, David Washington, Will Patterson, Jesse Owen, Jason Porter, Markus Kaulius, Matt Knox, Mitch Rice, Sean Madden, Jason Larson, Matt and Jen Mabe, Brent and Becky Stromme, Rob and Kimberly Skinner, Frank and Diane Clawson, Ricky and Miriam Verduzco and so many more—I love each of you deeply. Thank you for being part of my journey.

ACKNOWLEDGMENTS

To all the families who helped me through the challenges growing up—

You were lifelines, and your support mattered more than you know. Thank you.

To my Hitch Fit, SoulFIT Retreats, Breaker Mission, and CTN families—

Thank you. Your encouragement, belief, support, and love over the years has been monumental.

To the men who courageously shared their stories—Rob Elsey, Ben Richardson, and Ricardo Verduzco—thank you for allowing your transformation to be part of this message. Your honesty, vulnerability, and strength are a gift. I am honored to walk this journey with you. I love you all and blessed to call each of you family.

To the experts—Jessica Almond, Brent Stromme, Bryan Vignery, Candice Raine, Dr. Robert Rhoton, and the Arizona Trauma Institute—thank you for your invaluable insights, compassion, and dedication to the work of healing. Your expertise has deeply shaped and strengthened this mission.

To the teams at Forefront Publishing and Mission Driven Press—Thank you for helping bring this book to life with excellence. Your care and commitment helped turn this message into something that can now reach the world.

ENDNOTES

EPIGRAPH

1. The Holy Bible, *The Amplified Bible* (Grand Rapids, MI: Zondervan, 2015).

CHAPTER 9

2. B. Singh et al., "Effectiveness of Physical Activity Interventions for Improving Depression, Anxiety and Distress: An Overview of Systematic Reviews," *British Journal of Sports Medicine* 57 (2023): 1203–9.
3. Bruce D. Perry, "The Neurosequential Model of Therapeutics: Applying Principles of Neuroscience to Clinical Work with Traumatized and Maltreated Children," in *Working with Traumatized Youth in Child Welfare*, ed. N. Boyd Webb (New York: Guilford Press, 2005), 27–52.

CHAPTER 10

4. "Perpetrators of Sexual Violence: Statistics," Rape, Abuse and Incest National Network, https://rainn.org/statistics/perpetrators-sexual-violence.

CHAPTER 15

5. "Fraggle Rock Theme," by Philip Balsam and Dennis Lee, Spirit Two Music o/b/o Jim Henson Productions, 1983.

CHAPTER 21

6. "Forever," by Brian Johnson, Christa Black Gifford, Gabriel Wilson, Jenn Johnson, Joel Taylor, and Kari Jobe Carnes, lyrics © Sony/ATV Music Publishing LLC, Songtrust Ave, Bethel Music Publishing.
7. Cecil Murphey and Gary Roe, *Not Quite Healed: 40 Truths for Male Survivors of Childhood Sexual Abuse* (Grand Rapids, MI: Kregel Publications, 2013).

CHAPTER 26

8. The Holy Bible, *New International Version* (Grand Rapids, MI: Zondervan, 2011).

CHAPTER 30

9. The battle at Jericho is found in Joshua 6:1–27.

CHAPTER 32

10. The Holy Bible, *New International Version* (Grand Rapids, MI: Zondervan, 2011).

CHAPTER 34

11. The Holy Bible, *The Amplified Bible* (Grand Rapids, MI: Zondervan, 2015).
12. Ibid.
13. Isaiah 61:1, *The Bible in Basic English* (Cambridge Press, 1965). Public domain.
14. See also Luke 4:18–19.

CHAPTER 36

15. You'll find a list of courses and other helpful materials in the Resources section at the end of this book.

16. Substance Abuse and Mental Health Services Administration, *SAMHSA's Concept of Trauma and Guidance for a Trauma-Informed Approach* (Rockville, MD: U.S. Department of Health and Human Services, 2014). https://www.health.ny.gov/health_care/medicaid/program/medicaid_health_homes/docs/samhsa_trauma_concept_paper.pdf.
17. Tori Mae Hein.

CHAPTER 37

18. Andrew Ortiz, *Delayed Disclosure Factsheet: 2024* (Philadelphia, PA: CHILD USA, June 2024), https://childusa.org/wp-content/uploads/2024/06/Delayed-Disclosure-2024.pdf?
19. S. D. Easton et al., "'Would You Tell Under Circumstances Like That?': Barriers to Disclosure of Child Sexual Abuse for Men," *Psychology of Men & Masculinities* 15, no. 4 (2014): 460–69, https://doi.org/10.1037/a0034223.
20. Joe Tucci and Janise Mitchell, "Still Unseen & Ignored: Tracking Community Knowledge and Attitudes About Child Abuse and Child Protection in Australia," August 2021, Australian Childhood Foundation, https://www.childhood.org.au/app/uploads/2021/08/Still-unseen-and-ignored-report-FINAL-REPORT-17aug21.pdf.
21. Royal Commission into Institutional Responses to Child Sexual Abuse, *Final Report: Volume 3, Impacts* (Canberra, ACT: Royal Commission into Institutional Responses to Child Sexual Abuse, December 2017), https://www.childabuseroyalcommission.gov.au/sites/default/files/final_report_-_volume_3_impacts.pdf.
22. Centers for Disease Control and Prevention, "About Adverse Childhood Experiences," https://www.cdc.gov/aces/about/index.html
23. Scott D. Easton, "Masculine Norms, Disclosure, and Childhood Adversities Predict Long-Term Mental Distress among Men with Histories of Child Sexual Abuse," *Child Abuse & Neglect* 38, no. 2 (2014): 243-51, https://doi.org/10.1016/j.chiabu.2013.08.020.
24. "Tips for Talking with Survivors of Sexual Assault," Rape, Abuse and Incest National Network, https://rainn.org/articles/tips-talking-survivors-sexual-assault.

25. Bessel A. van der Kolk, *The Body Keeps the Score: Brain, Mind, and Body in the Healing of Trauma* (New York: Viking, 2014).

CHAPTER 38

26. Justin C. Strickland and Mark A. Smith, "The Anxiolytic Effects of Resistance Exercise," *Frontiers in Psychology* 5 (July 2014): 753, https://doi.org/10.3389/fpsyg.2014.00753; Michael Noetel et al., "Effect of Exercise for Depression: Systematic Review and Network Meta-analysis of Randomised Controlled Trials," *BMJ* (May 2024), https://doi.org/10.1136/bmj.q1024.
27. Ben Singh et al., "Effectiveness of Physical Activity Interventions for Improving Depression, Anxiety and Distress: An Overview of Systematic Reviews," *British Journal of Sports Medicine* 57 (2023): 1203–9, https://bjsm.bmj.com/content/57/18/1203.
28. Felice N. Jacka et al., "A Randomised Controlled Trial of Dietary Improvement for Adults with Major Depression (the 'SMILES' Trial)," *BMC Medicine* 15 no. 23 (2017), https://doi.org/10.1186/s12916-017-0791-y. Natalie Parletta et al., "A Mediterranean-Style Dietary Intervention Supplemented with Fish Oil Improves Diet Quality and Mental Health in People with Depression: A Randomized Controlled Trial (HELFIMED)," *Nutritional Neuroscience* 22, no. 7 (2017); 474–87, https://doi.org/10.1080/1028415X.2017.1411320.
29. Seth J. Gillihan, "Can the Right Diet Help You Heal from Trauma?," *Psychology Today*, December 9, 2019, https://www.psychologytoday.com/us/blog/think-act-be/201912/can-the-right-diet-help-you-heal-trauma.
30. Tricia Klassen, "Childhood Resilience and the Role of Rhythm," Crisis & Trauma Resource Institute, https://ctrinstitute.com/blog/childhood-resilience-rythym/.
31. Carolyn M. Fratto, "Trauma-Informed Care for Youth in Foster Care," *Archives of Psychiatric Nursing* 30, no. 3 (2016): 439–46, https://www.psychiatricnursing.org/article/S0883-9417(16)00017-0/abstract.
32. W. Li and X. Shen, "Research Progress in Trauma Metabolism and Nutrition," in *Advanced Trauma and Surgery*, ed. X. Fu and L. Liu

(Springer, 2017), https://doi.org/10.1007/978-981-10-2425-2_10. Alessandra Borges et al., "Nutritional Therapy in Trauma," in *The Trauma Golden Hour*, ed. Nasr Adonis et al. (Springer, 2020), 221–26, https://link.springer.com/chapter/10.1007/978-3-030-26443-7_41.

33. W. Li and X. Shen, "Research Progress in Trauma Metabolism and Nutrition," in *Advanced Trauma and Surgery*, ed. X. Fu and L. Liu (Springer, 2017), https://doi.org/10.1007/978-981-10-2425-2_10.

34. Divine Nwafor et al., "Nutritional Support Following Traumatic Brain Injury: A Comprehensive Review," *Exploratory Research and Hypothesis in Medicine* 8, no. 3 (2023): 236–47, doi: 10.14218/ERHM.2022.00086.

35. Stephanie Strachan and Karen Friend, "Nutrition in the Critically Injured Patient," in *Trauma and Combat Critical Care in Clinical Practice*, ed. Sam Hutchings (Springer, 2016), 425–64.

36. Kara Wittholz, Kate Fetterplace, Melinda Clode, Emma S. George, Carolyn M. MacIsaac, Rachael Judson, John J. Presneill, and Adam M. Deane, "Measuring Nutrition-Related Outcomes in a Cohort of Multi-Trauma Patients Following Intensive Care Unit Discharge," *Journal of Human Nutrition and Dietetics* 33, no. 3 (June 2020): 414–22, https://doi.org/10.1111/jhn.12719

37. Asad Azim et al., "Early Feeds Not Force Feeds: Enteral Nutrition in Traumatic Brain Injury," *Journal of Trauma and Acute Care Surgery* 81, no. 3 (2016): 520–24, doi: 10.1097/TA.0000000000001089.

CHAPTER 39

38. Kimberly Matheson, Ajani Asokumar, and Hymie Anisman, "Resilience: Safety in the Aftermath of Traumatic Stressor Experiences," *Frontiers in Behavioral Neuroscience* 14 (2020): Article 596919, https://doi.org/10.3389/fnbeh.2020.596919

39. Ian Sarinopoulos, Daniel W. Grupe, Katie L. Mackiewicz, John D. Herrington, Miriam Lör, Emma E. Steege, and Jack B. Nitschke, "Uncertainty during Anticipation Modulates Neural Responses to Aversion in Human Insula and Amygdala," *Cerebral Cortex* 20, no. 4 (April 2010): 929–940, https://doi.org/10.1093/cercor/bhp155

40. Kimberly Matheson, Ajani Asokumar, and Hymie Anisman, "Resilience: Safety in the Aftermath of Traumatic Stressor Experiences," *Frontiers in Behavioral Neuroscience* 14 (2020): Article 596919, https://doi.org/10.3389/fnbeh.2020.596919

41. University of California San Francisco, Langley Porter Psychiatric Hospital & Clinics, *Emotion Regulation Skills Manual* (San Francisco: University of California San Francisco, n.d.), https://psychiatry.ucsf.edu/sites/psych.ucsf.edu/files/EMOTION%20REGULATION%20SKILLS%20MANUAL.pdf

42. Matthias Domhardt, Annika Münzer, Jörg M. Fegert, and Lutz Goldbeck, "Resilience in Survivors of Child Sexual Abuse: A Systematic Review of the Literature," *Trauma, Violence, & Abuse* 16, no. 4 (October 2015): 476–93, https://doi.org/10.1177/1524838014557288

43. Zoe Chouliara, Tony Karatzias, and Athena Gullone, "Recovering from Childhood Sexual Abuse: A Theoretical Framework for Practice and Research," *Journal of Psychiatric & Mental Health Nursing* 21, no. 1 (2014): 69-78, https://doi.org/10.1111/jpm.12048

CHAPTER 40

44. The Holy Bible, *New International Version*®, NIV®. Copyright © 1973, 1978, 1984, 2011 by Biblica, Inc.® Used by permission of Zondervan. All rights reserved worldwide.

CHAPTER 41

45. The Holy Bible, *English Standard Version* (Wheaton, IL: Crossway Bibles, 2016).

46. The Holy Bible, *New International Version* (Grand Rapids, MI: Zondervan, 2011).

47. Ibid.

48. Ibid.

CHAPTER 42

49. The Holy Bible, *English Standard Version*. ESV® Text Edition: 2016. Copyright © 2001 by Crossway Bibles, a publishing ministry of Good News Publishers.
50. This quote is often attributed to Rory Vaden. See "How to Find Your Ideal Client," *Rory Vaden* (blog), https://roryvaden.com/blog/sales/how-do-you-find-your-ideal-client/.

ABOUT MICAH LACERTE

Micah LaCerte is a world champion fitness athlete, entrepreneur, speaker, author, *Iron Man Magazine* cover model, and transformation coach with over twenty-five years of experience guiding individuals to lasting change. He is the cofounder of Hitch Fit Online Personal Training and Hitch Fit Gym, where he and his wife, Diana Chaloux-LaCerte, have helped clients in eighty-two countries lose over 750,000 pounds through fully customized, life-changing programs.

Micah has been a trusted leader in the fitness industry for decades, featured across national media outlets and live stages. He and Diana also cofounded SoulFIT Retreats—powerful experiences that blend faith, fitness, and fun to help others heal and create lasting transformation.

Micah is the founder of The Breaker Mission, a movement dedicated to helping men overcome shame, pain, and past trauma, enabling them to walk in freedom and purpose.

Motivated by his deep faith in and relationship with Jesus Christ, Micah is passionate about using his platform to serve. For over a decade, he and Diana have supported a school in Haiti, providing education and care for more than eighty children each month.

He lives in Kansas City with his wife, Diana, where they continue their mission to transform lives around the world—physically, mentally, emotionally, and spiritually.